P9-CJD-459

THE FIRST AMERICANS

✣

Other Publications:

WEIGHT WATCHERS® SMART CHOICE RECIPE COLLECTION
TRUE CRIME
THE ART OF WOODWORKING
LOST CIVILIZATIONS
ECHOES OF GLORY
THE NEW FACE OF WAR
HOW THINGS WORK
WINGS OF WAR
CREATIVE EVERYDAY COOKING
COLLECTOR'S LIBRARY OF THE UNKNOWN
CLASSICS OF WORLD WAR II
TIME-LIFE LIBRARY OF CURIOUS AND UNUSUAL FACTS
AMERICAN COUNTRY
VOYAGE THROUGH THE UNIVERSE
THE THIRD REICH
THE TIME-LIFE GARDENER'S GUIDE
MYSTERIES OF THE UNKNOWN
TIME FRAME
FIX IT YOURSELF
FITNESS, HEALTH & NUTRITION
SUCCESSFUL PARENTING
HEALTHY HOME COOKING
UNDERSTANDING COMPUTERS
LIBRARY OF NATIONS
THE ENCHANTED WORLD
THE KODAK LIBRARY OF CREATIVE PHOTOGRAPHY
GREAT MEALS IN MINUTES
THE CIVIL WAR
PLANET EARTH
COLLECTOR'S LIBRARY OF THE CIVIL WAR
THE EPIC OF FLIGHT
THE GOOD COOK
WORLD WAR II
HOME REPAIR AND IMPROVEMENT
THE OLD WEST

For information on and a full description of any of the Time-Life Books series listed above, please call 1-800-621-7026 or write:
Reader Information
Time-Life Customer Service
P.O. Box C-32068
Richmond, Virginia 23261-2068

This volume is one of a series that chronicles the history and culture of the Native Americans. Other books in the series include:

THE SPIRIT WORLD
THE EUROPEAN CHALLENGE
PEOPLE OF THE DESERT
THE WAY OF THE WARRIOR

The Cover: Although the first Americans left no written records, artifacts such as this hammered copper profile of a warrior excavated from an earthen burial mound in Oklahoma establish that sophisticated cultures flourished on the continent long before Europeans arrived. The object, some seven centuries old, was originally part of a larger ceremonial headdress.

THE FIRST AMERICANS

by
THE EDITORS
of
TIME-LIFE BOOKS

ALEXANDRIA, VIRGINIA

Second printing 1993. Printed in U.S.A.
Published simultaneously in Canada.
School and library distribution by Silver Burdett Company, Morristown, New Jersey 07960.

Library of Congress Cataloging in Publication Data
The First Americans/by the editors of Time-Life Books.
p. cm. — (The American Indians)
Includes bibliographical references.
ISBN 0-8094-9400-0
ISBN 0-8094-9401-9 (lib. bdg.)
1. Indians of North America—Origin.
2. Indians of North America—History.
I. Time-Life Books. II. Series.
E61.F56 1992 92-6548
970.01'1—dc20 CIP

General Consultants
Frederick E. Hoxie is director of the D'Arcy McNickle Center for the History of the American Indian at the Newberry Library in Chicago. Dr. Hoxie is the author of *A Final Promise: The Campaign to Assimilate the Indians 1880-1920* and other works. He has served as a history consultant to the Cheyenne River and Standing Rock Sioux tribes, Little Big Horn College archives, and the Senate Select Committee on Indian Affairs. He is a trustee of the National Museum of the American Indian in Washington, D.C.

Dean R. Snow, Professor of Anthropology at the University at Albany SUNY, has written numerous archaeological books and articles, including *Archaeology of New England* and the *Atlas of Ancient America,* which he coauthored. Dr. Snow is a member of the Society for American Archaeology and a fellow of the American Association for the Advancement of Science. He is currently involved in the Mohawk Valley Project, a demographic archaeological study of the rise and decline of the Mohawk nation and an operation to salvage its artifacts.

Special Consultants
Frank and A. J. Bock are archaeologists who have devoted much of their professional life to the study and preservation of North American Indian rock art, spending many summers on the Hopi and Navajo reservations. The Bocks founded and are charter members of The American Rock Art Research Association.

Linda S. Cordell is Curator and Chairman of the Department of Anthropology at the California Academy of Sciences in San Francisco. She has directed archaeological research in New Mexico for many years and is the author of *Prehistory of the Southwest.*

Donald Mitchell is a professor in the Department of Anthropology at the University of Victoria in British Columbia, Canada. He has done extensive archaeological work throughout British Columbia as well as ethnological research on the economies of the Northwest Coast.

Vincas Petras Steponaitis, Director of the Research Laboratories of Anthropology at the University of North Carolina, specializes in the archaeology of the eastern United States. He is President of the Southern Archaeological Conference, a board member of the Society for American Archaeology, and a former editor of *Southeast Archaeology.*

CONTENTS

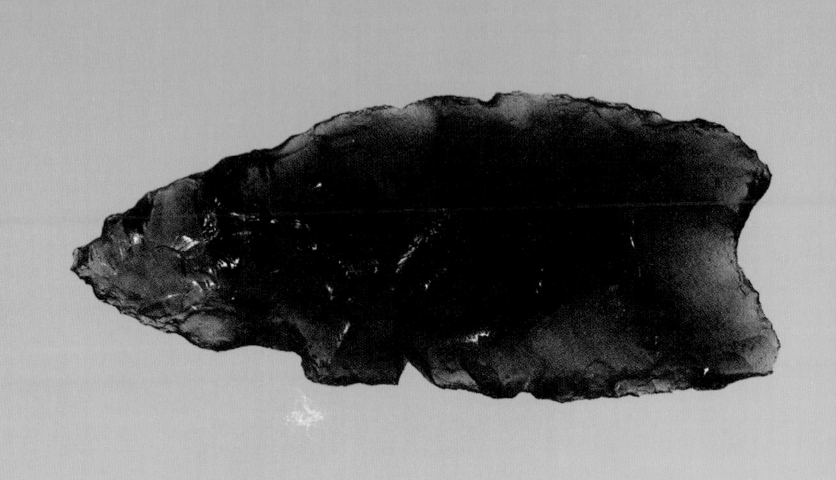

1

TRAILBLAZERS IN A NEW WORLD

Awash with Arctic sunlight, the Brooks Range in central Alaska looks much as it did thousands of years ago when America's first inhabitants crossed the Bering land bridge, probably in pursuit of big game. These New World hunters developed an array of simple weapons that included an obsidian spearpoint (above, left) discovered near Alaska's Koyukuk River.

Clad in warm fur and armed with cold chiseled stone, they were about to embark on an epic journey of discovery. Behind them stretched the barrens of Siberia, where their ancestors had clung to existence in the depths of the Ice Age, pursuing prey across treeless plains scoured by fierce Arctic winds. Ahead lay the unmarked frontier of an immeasurable continent—a labyrinthine wilderness that would lure generations of their descendants down a thousand strange paths.

The resourceful Asian nomads who made this pioneering trek to America ages before European explorers dreamed of its existence never paused to savor their accomplishment. Indeed, they had no way of distinguishing the new world they were entering from the old one they were leaving behind. So much of the earth's water had been locked up in glaciers during the Ice Age that sea levels had dropped, exposing a broad corridor of tundra between Siberia and Alaska, home to herds of great mammals. Onto this beckoning bridge stalked the first Americans.

Unlike Christopher Columbus and other shrewd adventurers who would subsequently descend on American shores lusting for gold and glory, these Asian pioneers sought only the humblest of earthly rewards—food, clothing, and shelter, much of which they derived from big game, such as the woolly mammoth, by consuming the flesh of their prey, donning the hides, and using the bones to build huts. Nonetheless, the simple act of tracking quarry across the land bridge launched the nameless wanderers on one of the greatest exploits in human history. Over a period of time, their descendants would follow the migratory herds southward into more temperate latitudes, fanning out across a virgin continent. For countless generations, those original Americans would continue to subsist principally by hunting, wielding similar weapons and pursuing much the same strategies from one region to another. Ultimately, however, alterations in the environment would compel many bands to confine themselves to discrete areas and adopt ways of living that were tailored to those habitats. On seacoast and plain, in desert and forest, people would

A NAKOAKTOK CHIEF

AN APACHE CHIEF

Photographed during the early twentieth century, descendants of the first Americans show physical aspects of a shared inheritance. The variety of clothing, jewelry, and accouterments pictured on these pages, however, attests to the rich mixture of cultures and lifestyles that blossomed from the earliest nomadic bands who crossed the land bridge from Asia into the New World.

eventually form distinct societies to hunt, fish, forage, and often grow their own food at permanent settlements, where they would lay the foundations of long-lasting cultures.

For all the diversity of the first Americans, they inherited certain common traits from their Old World ancestors. Reflecting their Asiatic heritage, they were generally of short to medium stature, with straight black hair, light brown skin, and prominent cheekbones—features that in 1492 reinforced Columbus's mistaken conviction that he had reached the East Indies and prompted him to assign to the inhabitants the inaccurate yet enduring title of Indians. Of the approximately 300 languages that were spoken by North American Indians when Columbus reached the New World, the vast majority were derived from an ancestral tongue known as Amerind, carried to America by the first wave of travelers over the land bridge. Two subsequent migrations—the last of which must have been undertaken by boat after the Ice Age ended and the land bridge was swallowed up by the rising sea—endowed the New World with smaller language groups: one spoken by Athapaskan peoples, including the Navajo and Apache, who eventually reached the American Southwest shortly before the arrival of the Europeans; and the other by the Aleuts and Inuit of Alaska and northwestern Canada, whose ancestors took part in the most recent exodus from Siberia.

Divided as they were by language and custom, neighboring Indian tribes sometimes clashed in tests of arms that compelled the losers to flee

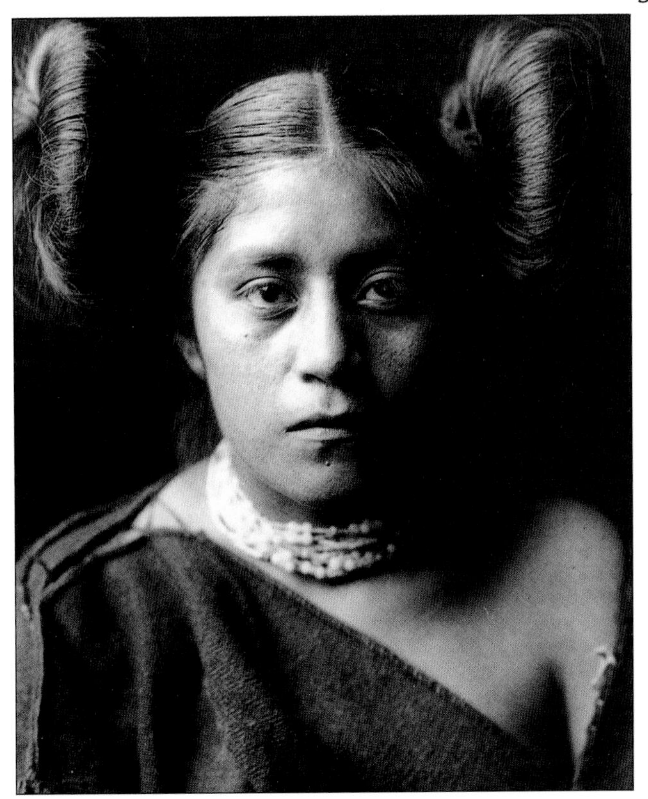

A TEWA GIRL

AN ATSINA WARRIOR

or be subjugated. But not even the toughest and most warlike of the New World peoples were prepared for the struggle that began with the arrival of European colonists, who challenged the Indians not only with firearms and cunning policies but also with invisible scourges that sometimes overcame the defenses of entire nations. As the frontier advanced, the survivors fought gallantly to stem the European tide. With few exceptions, the Indians were forced to give way, but they managed to preserve communities where their rich heritage lives on. Gradually, Americans whose ancestors arrived in recent centuries have come to understand that their own history in the New World amounts to a brief episode compared with the drama played out there by the Indians over an expanse of time stretching back far beyond the founding of the earliest civilizations of the Old World.

The reconstruction of that extensive record has been difficult due to the fact that the first Americans did not develop written languages. Nevertheless, they told their compelling story in legends and in pictures, in clay and in stone, and much of what they left behind them has been interpreted with the assistance of their descendants. In the final analysis, the tale is not one of defeat, for in spirit the Indians never sought to subdue the land and could not surrender it. Rather, they recognized the earth as a great power in its own right and came to terms with it, conforming their pursuits to the requirements of nature in ways from which those who claim title to the land today could learn a great deal.

AN APSAROKE WARRIOR

A WISHRAM BRIDE

The peopling of the New World represented the culmination of an ancient migratory process in which humans progressively mastered ever-harsher climes. More than 40,000 years ago, the anatomically modern human beings known as *Homo sapiens sapiens* spread out from tropical Africa into Europe and Asia, where they replaced an earlier species, the Neanderthals. This expansion occurred during the most recent phase of the Ice Age—a glaciation that began at least 80,000 years ago and ended scarcely 10,000 years ago. During that long siege, there were occasional lulls when the icecaps retreated and the climate moderated. But conditions were never less than forbidding in the far north. Undeterred, modern humans entered that stringent environment in pursuit of sustenance, reaching present-day Siberia perhaps 35,000 years ago.

That they survived and even prospered in such a punishing place was due in part to the presence of herds of meaty mammals that were well adapted to the cold, and in good measure to the human knack for developing tools and technologies to extract the most from limited resources. Mammoths, muskoxen, and woolly rhinoceroses were just a few of the species that grazed voraciously on herbage across the plains of Siberia during the summer and conserved the acquired energy beneath thick pelts through the long winters. Hunters exploited such quarry with tremendous efficiency, seldom allowing even the skeletons to go to waste. The bones of the beasts not only provided the framework for hide-covered shelters but also were carved into perforated needles that the

A KWAKIUTL CHIEF

A PAPAGO WOMAN

nomads then threaded with sinews to sew layered garments of animal skin that provided protection against sub-zero cold.

Among the people who ranged into Siberia during the late stages of the Ice Age were nomads from what is now northern China, who made the journey with an impressive repertoire of stone tools, including spearheads carefully flaked on both sides to yield a point that could penetrate thick hides and large axes with which to butcher big game. These well-prepared hunters may have been the immediate antecedents of the American Indians. Eventually, some of the hunters wandered farther to the north and east in search of fresh quarry—by one estimate, the fauna of the region could support only about one person per square mile. As the nomadic vanguard approached the Arctic Circle, they happened upon the land bridge to the New World.

Exactly when humans first crossed that corridor remains a matter of conjecture. It was exposed two or three times during the latest epoch of glaciation when the expanding icecaps bound up enough moisture on a global scale to uncover the land beneath the shallow Bering Strait separating Siberia from Alaska. The land bridge may have been passable from the time humans first reached Siberia until about 32,000 years ago, when an interglacial lull commenced. If so, some nomads could have crossed then and filtered southward, which may explain tantalizing signs of human activity in the New World that have been tentatively dated as far back as 20,000 to 30,000 years ago. But such indications are sparse com-

A LUMMI WOMAN

A ZUNI GOVERNOR

pared with the abundant evidence of a decisive and far-reaching migration that began approximately 15,000 years ago, when a glacial resurgence had covered nearly one-third of the earth's surface with ice and lowered sea levels fully 300 feet.

At that time, the land bridge was so broad it formed a distinctive subcontinent, which has been dubbed Beringia. Extending several hundred miles to the north and south of the present-day Bering Strait, Beringia included the eastern tip of Siberia and a substantial portion of Alaska. Thanks in part to the moderating influence of Pacific Ocean currents, this corridor remained largely free of ice. At the same time, however, massive glaciers covered the mountainous Pacific rim of Alaska and Canada and North America's frigid heartland, blocking the further advance of man and beast until the ice receded.

Like the land the nomads left behind, Beringia was bereft of trees, raked by savage winds, and gripped during the winter by sub-zero temperatures even lower than those of today. Yet in summer, when the sun remained above the horizon for all but a few hours at most, the region was transformed into a verdant marshland that may have offered more nourishment to animal life than does modern tundra. Carpeted with a variety of plants, from sedges and grasses to willow shrub, it sustained large herds of caribou and a variety of hulking herbivores that have since become extinct, including the giant bison, with horns that spanned six feet; and several species of mammoths, towering up to twelve feet tall at the

A NEZ PERCÉ MAN

A CAYUGA CHIEF

shoulders and equipped with skirtlike fringes of fur that shielded their vitals against the elements and broad padlike feet that allowed them to roam marshy pastures without bogging down. Preying on the grass eaters were long-fanged carnivores such as the dire wolf, which human predators faced at their peril.

Profiting by their Siberian heritage, the people of Beringia dealt resourcefully with the rigors of their environment. Stalking the herds would have been difficult in the depths of winter, so the Beringians may have stockpiled meat by drying and freezing it, enabling them to hunker down by the fire inside their shelters when the dark season descended. They may also have preserved berries and other summertime forage, yet they relied mainly on meat, not only for protein but also for vitamins and other essential nutrients. To keep flames flickering through the months of scant sunlight, the Beringians probably fueled their hearths with dried dung in the absence of brush or timber.

After supporting this type of existence for many generations, Beringia literally underwent a sea change. Here, as in Siberia, the human population gradually expanded and the herds of big herbivores dwindled. But that was a minor challenge compared with the upheaval that occurred around 12,000 BC when the planet began to warm up. As the glaciers melted and retreated, huge volumes of water that had been bound up in ice were liberated. Sea levels rose, nibbling at the fringes of Beringia and reducing its sparse pastures. Under the pressure, some Beringians may have retreated westward back into Siberia. Within a millennium or two, the land bridge was severed by the rising waters, and the Bering Strait became an enduring divide between the Old World and the New.

If some Beringians ended up back in the Old World, many others pushed ahead as the Ice Age waned, advancing through central Alaska and the Yukon. An inviting corridor between two daunting mountain chains—the Alaska Range to the south and the Brooks Range to the north—made it possible for humans and the animals they preyed on to advance all the way to the Mackenzie River valley in northwestern Canada, a gateway to the low-lying interior of the continent. There, the continuing warming of the planet brought the migrants a great bonus. To the south, a gap was opening between two icecaps that once had formed an impenetrable block—one covering western North America from the Rocky Mountains to the Pacific and reaching from lower Alaska to present-day Washington State, and the other engulfing the eastern two-thirds of the continent down to a line defined today roughly by the Missouri and Ohio rivers. Every year, the gap between the two glaciers widened a bit along the eastern flank of the Rocky Mountains, and bold exiles from Beringia exploited that opening. Once again, it was the tracks of their prey—herds of mammoth and great bison—that lured humans ever deeper into the unknown.

This journey southward probably began around 11,000 BC. Before that, the ice-free alley would have been less than twenty-five miles wide, creating impossibly cruel conditions of cold and wind. The migration through the widening corridor in all likelihood took centuries, as each generation moved south at the rate of a few miles a year. Then, more than 1,500 miles from their Mackenzie Valley starting point, the human vanguard broke through onto the Great Plains, an emergent grassland stretching southward from the present-day Dakotas for hundreds of miles. As they spread out across prairie and woodland, the nomads encountered startling evidence that they had indeed entered a strange new world—a fabulous assortment of wild creatures that had long haunted the Ameri-

Only three miles of water, the shallow Bering Strait, separates Alaska's Little Diomede Island (below, left) and Siberia's Big Diomede Island shown in the background at right. During the Ice Age, however, (map, right) so much of the earth's water was frozen in glaciers (light blue) that the sea level was drastically lowered, uncovering a vast land bridge (light gray) that provided a direct route to North America for herds of game and bands of migrating hunters.

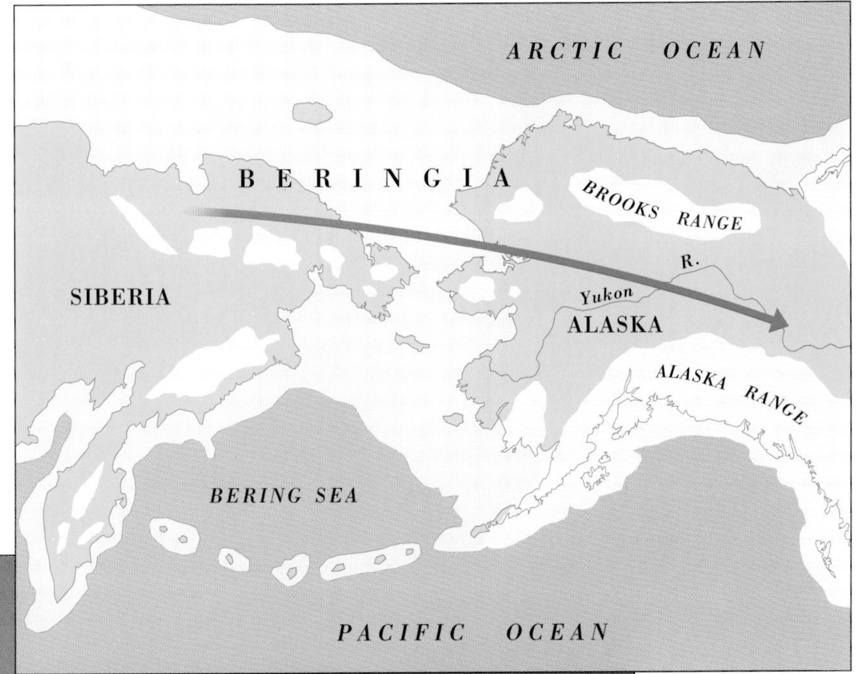

can wilderness, including beavers as big as bears, nearly seven feet long with eight-inch incisors; and giant ground sloths, weighing close to three tons and rising more than fifteen feet on their hind legs. Undaunted by animals that towered over them, the human hunters incorporated the more palatable of these prodigies into their diet.

Now that their migrations were no longer constrained by ice, the nomads found tempting prospects beckoning them from every direction. Some of them headed east through lush river valleys toward the Atlantic Ocean; others filed through passes in the Rocky Mountains to the Pacific; many continued southward across the ocean of grass. By 10,000 BC Indians were ensconced in Middle America—a fertile area extending from the Rio Grande to the Panamanian isthmus. By 9000 BC humans riding the crest of the great migratory wave fetched up at the southernmost tip of South America, Tierra del Fuego—a distance of some 8,000 miles from the original entryway in Beringia.

Across the length and breadth of North America, the descendants of the nomads who swept down from the Arctic pursued a relatively consistent way of life that underwent small but significant changes over the generations. For thousands of years, these Indians, similar to their forebears in Siberia and Beringia, continued to support themselves primarily by hunting, moving about in small bands that traveled light, with animal skins for protection against the elements and weapons and tools made of stone and bone for killing and processing game. Occasionally, however, sheer ingenuity or modifications in the environment propelled early hunters to alter the tools of their trade. They de-

veloped new projectile points and deployed them in distinctive ways that defined their cultures.

The first of these Indian cultures was the Clovis, named for a town in present-day New Mexico where hunters tracking prey around 9500 BC left distinctive spearpoints amid the bones of their favorite target, a mammoth. Similar points have been found at sites throughout the Great Plains with the remains of various other species, including bison, camels, and horses. These Clovis people were probably the original hunters of the grasslands, who improved on the stone weaponry of their ancestors and soon carried their know-how to other parts of the continent. Within a few hundred years, human predators in modern-day Nova Scotia were hurling Clovis points at caribou on the tundra some sixty miles south of the ebbing eastern icecap. In forests to the south, meanwhile, hunters equipped with a similar cutting edge may have included among their prey the mastodon, an elephant-like creature similar to the mammoth but adapted to browsing in the shade rather than grazing in the open.

The hallmark of Clovis culture was a stone spearhead that ranged in length from three to six inches and tapered like a laurel leaf from a broad, blunt base to a sharp point. Following the lead of their Siberian ancestors, Clovis stonecutters flaked this blade smooth on both sides to reduce resistance to its thrust. But they added a handy touch of their own by chipping a central channel, or flute, on at least one side and usually both, extending at least one-third of the way from the base to the tip. Although wooden spear shafts used by Clovis hunters have not survived intact, the

Beringian hunters disguised as caribou plan an attack on a herd migrating through the spring snow. Caribou supplied many products—meat and fat for food, hides for warm clothing, sinews for thread, and bones and antlers from which ancient Indians made everything from skin scrapers to needles.

flute on the spearpoint must have allowed it to fit snugly into the notched end of the shaft, where the point was then secured with a lashing of sinews. By strengthening the link between shaft and spearhead, fluting represented a major advance in hunting technology—perhaps the first such innovation to occur on American soil.

The likely site of this invention—the Great Plains—was a hunter's paradise. Semiarid today, the region then benefited from the presence of the ice to the north, which produced somewhat cooler and wetter summers. Ponds and rivers lured thirsty ruminants, while deep-rooted grasses offered the creatures nourishment late into the year. To reap the animal bounty, early hunters in all probability employed their Clovis-tipped spears in two ways—casting them like javelins or thrusting them in at close quarters like lances. Unlike later projectile tips, the Clovis points were not equipped with barbs that stuck in the flesh of the animal. Instead, these hunters dispatched their prey with repeated thrusts of their weapons. Alternatively, some throwing spears were evidently rigged with detachable bone foreshafts that broke off when the point lodged in the target. The hunter then could quickly rearm his spear with a new foreshaft and resume his attack. Once the animal fell, the detachable foreshaft could be employed as a knife, complete with handle, for skinning and cutting up the prize.

The fortunes of the hunters would have been considerably enhanced if, as appears likely, the Clovis weaponry included that ingenious spear-thrower known as an atlatl: a shaft of wood or bone perhaps two feet long with a handle at one end and a hooked tip at the other that fit into the notched butt end of the spear. Grasping the spear with thumb and forefinger and the handle of the atlatl with the other three fingers, the hunter flung the spear with a snap of his wrist. This whipping motion, enhanced by the effective lengthening of the hunter's arm, enabled him to deliver the spear with greater speed, range, and impact. The atlatl was invented in Eurasia at least 5,000 years before the Clovis period and was still being employed against the Spanish invaders more than 10,000 years afterward by the Aztecs of Mexico, who gave the device its name. More perishable than the stone points they propelled, atlatls have not been recovered from Clovis sites, but the Indians of that time may well have inherited the useful instrument from their Siberian ancestors or perhaps developed it on their own.

Even with the assistance of the atlatl, however, the mammoth must have been a formidable foe, protected both by its redoubtable physique

Preserved in a piece of clay found near present-day Folsom, New Mexico, a 10,000-year-old, finely chipped spearpoint remains lodged between the ribs of a giant bison. Even older points, those belonging to the Clovis culture, have been discovered among both bison and mammoth bones across much of the North American continent.

and by its group instincts. Weighing as much as ten tons and brandishing eight-foot-long tusks, the beast deterred a casual approach. Its inch-thick skin slowed the penetration of even the sharp Clovis point. And, like modern elephants, all mammoths except mature males almost surely clustered in herds led by a matriarch. The beasts were hampered by poor eyesight but had excellent hearing and a keen sense of smell. Hunters never knew when a herd of a dozen or more mammoths incited by an enraged matriarch might turn on them. The details of these fierce encounters have been reconstructed from the remains of butchered mammoths as well as from analogous kills by spear-wielding elephant hunters in modern Africa. Far from attacking impulsively, the mammoth stalkers might follow their prey for days on end until a vulnerable member of the herd—one of the younger or less vigorous animals, perhaps—strayed from the protection of the group. Then the predators pounced, overcoming their massive foe by means of a coordinated effort. One hunter might draw the attention of the beast, for example, while a companion worked around to the side and let fly with a spear.

Many Clovis kills occurred close to watering places. Already-wounded and feverish mammoths may have sought water, only to be finished off there or to drop from exhaustion. Others probably were slowed down by the muck and attacked before they could work their way out of

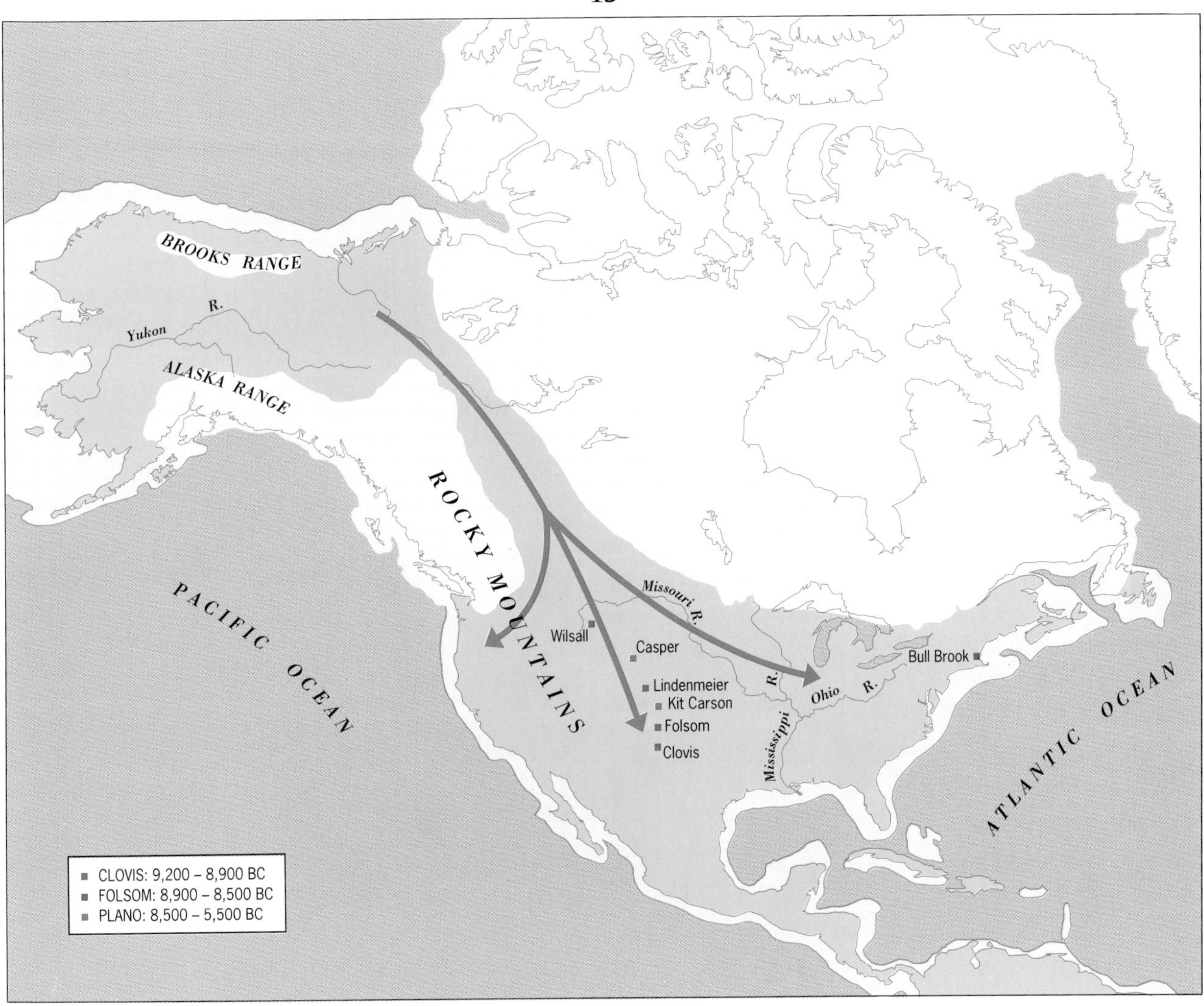

As the Ice Age waned and the glaciers that had covered southern Alaska and Canada receded, the first Americans ventured into the heart of the continent. After traveling down an ice-free corridor east of the Rocky Mountains, they dispersed eastward to the river valleys at midcontinent, westward through the Rockies, and southward into Middle America and beyond (arrows). Projectile points made by these first settlers have been discovered at the locations shown on the map. Such sites were ancient burial grounds, quarries, encampments, or places at which game was killed.

the dangerous area. Hunters sometimes set up camp on high ground overlooking ponds and streams that were frequented by the herds and waited there to ambush them. A mammoth required more than fifty gallons of water daily, and one could be expected to arrive eventually.

For the patient hunters, long days of tedium spent stalking or lying in wait for their prey culminated in a tableau of great drama and frenzy. Trapped in a marsh and surrounded by hunters, the mammoth trumpeted in rage as its tormentors unleashed spears from short range. Gradually, the beast weakened, its tusks and trunk flailing about in desperation. Some of the men shouted to distract it, while others approached from behind to slash at the muscles and tendons of the rear legs with sharp stone knives. Still others dashed in to jab at the stomach and chest, probing for the animal's lungs and foot-long heart. Then, mortally wounded, the mammoth collapsed, and its attackers pulled back and waited for death to come to the bloodstained marsh.

The most effective way to butcher the carcass was with two-person teams. While one pulled on a piece of flesh to maintain tension, the other wielded a stone knife sharpened to a razoredge to strip away the skin and cut steaks. One of the butchers sometimes crawled inside the carcass to remove favored internal organs, such as the heart or liver, leaving cut marks on the ribs as a legacy of the eerie journey. Someone might break open a leg bone and, using a stone scraper or bone fragment, dig out the highly nutritious marrow; later, when it was heated, the marrow would yield large quantities of buttery fat. In the meantime, helpers scraped flesh and fat from the thick skin of the beast with a variety of implements. Butchers often selected only those choice parts that were readily accessible. The carcass was so enormous and unwieldy that they could not turn it over to get to the meat on the other side. A single carcass, in any event, typically provided more flesh than a small band could transport and consume—even a modest six-ton mammoth might yield more than two tons of edible products.

A Pueblo Indian prepares to hurl a spear with the aid of an atlatl, or spear-thrower. The simple device (opposite) gave the hunter more power and extended the range of his projectile.

The hunters and their dependents consumed as much meat as possible while it was fresh, cooking it in wide, shallow firepits. Some of the meat was dried in strips of jerky for later consumption, but Clovis bands evidently did not possess elaborate techniques for the storage and preservation of food. As nomads, they were limited in any case to what they could carry with them. Meat could be transported in lightweight containers made from the skin of the butchered animal. The simplest carrying case was the animal's intact stomach—an edible pouch that could be heated over the fire at mealtime and consumed along with the contents.

Clovis people did not live by bulky mammals alone. Small versions of their fluted spearpoints found their marks in fowl, fish, rabbits, and other compact creatures that could be eaten at a single sitting. In addition, plant foods such as nuts, berries, fruits, seeds, and edible roots were there for the taking on the Great Plains and in other temperate regions. But as long as the giant herbivores remained abundant, Clovis bands did not have to divert too much of their energy to the time-consuming pursuit of forage. Generation after generation, they counted on big kills—perhaps a mammoth a year for each member of the band—to see them through.

The prosperity of Clovis hunters hinged on the quality of their stone weapons, which brought them not only nourishment but all the other animal-based raw materials they needed, such as hides, sinew, bone, ivory, and antler. Accordingly, they prospected diligently for the best sources of chert, jasper, chalcedony, and other fine-grained stone that could be worked to a sharp edge without fracturing. The discovery of a new source of high-quality stone by a hunting party must have been an occasion for celebration, for it would support the group's own requirements indefinitely and furnish material of the utmost value for exchange with others. Many such quarries were exploited for thousands of years.

Once found, quarries became regular stops on the seasonal rounds of some migratory bands. Hunters in eastern Pennsylvania used Onondaga flint obtained more than 200 miles away in New York's Susquehanna Valley, while bands seeking prey in New York carried chert that had been quarried in Ohio. Those who quarried the stone did not always complete their points on the spot; in some cases, miners prepared blanks, or preforms—flakes of the approximate length and thickness they desired for their spearheads. The preforms were then carried along by the hunters, who finished them as needed.

Clovis prospectors apparently prized certain kinds of stone for their alluring color or texture as well as their chipping properties. Perhaps hunters believed that a beautiful cutting edge would please their prey or

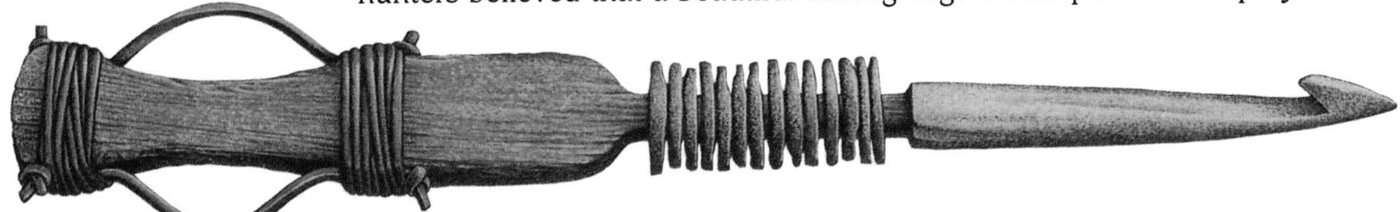

About two feet long, the atlatl had a blunt hook at one end to hold the butt of the spear. Leather loops at the other end afforded the hunter a firm grip, and stone weights in the middle likely provided balance.

the gods who presided over such matters. As befit instruments used to draw blood, red points were much sought after. Stoneworkers learned that one fine grade of eastern jasper turned a deep red when heated—an operation that improved the chipping qualities of the stone even as it endowed the point with a special significance.

Making stone points was the consummate art of the Clovis people. Their nomadic way of life evidently left little time or occasion for the kind

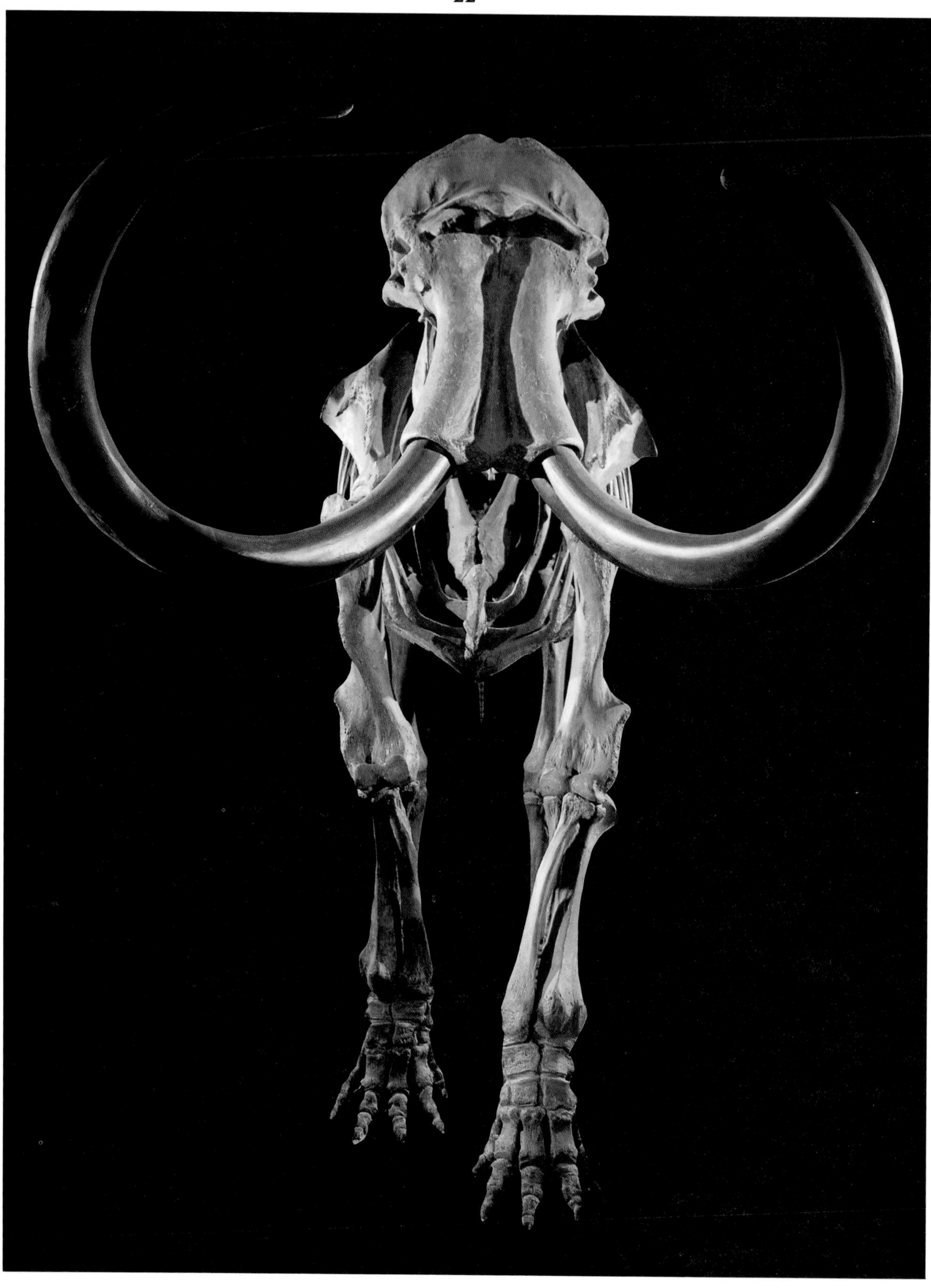

of cave painting or carving of figurines found in the Old World. But Clovis stoneworkers, or knappers, demonstrated a dexterity seldom equaled in ancient times. Step by step, they fashioned projectile points through percussion or pressure methods that trimmed away stone. The knapper might strike the stone directly with another stone or press down on a punch made of bone or antler. Removal of channel flakes to produce the distinctive Clovis fluting required a precise touch. Too much pressure or percussion would fracture the thin stone and force the craftsman to start over again with a new piece. The final step was to dull the edges on either side of the fluting near the base of the point so that the sinews that bound it to the spear shaft would not be cut to shreds.

The organizing principle of each Clovis band was most likely kinship, with the typical party consisting of no more than fifty members of a single extended family. Judging by the makeup of nomadic hunting societies in more recent times, this group probably consisted of males linked by blood relationships, along with their wives and children. All mature members of the band may have had some say in its affairs, but the ultimate authority most likely rested with males deemed leaders by virtue of their age, courage, or wisdom.

Teams of men probably ranged far afield to stalk the mighty mammoth. Once they had slain the beast, a messenger would notify the rest of the band. Women and children would move up to the kill, and the entire party would remain there, camping in caves, skin-covered shelters, or simple windbreaks of brush until the supply of fresh meat was exhausted. Then, the band would pack up their sparse possessions and move on to a new campsite or an old one, in a ritual that might be repeated on scores of occasions each year.

Ties of kinship extended beyond the individual band. Males probably remained members of the bands into which they were born, a practice that would have enabled them to hunt familiar territory in cooperation with the companions they knew best—their fathers, uncles, brothers, and sons. Women, on the other hand, were most likely sent off to marry into neighboring bands in exchange for mates for their brothers and male cousins—a practice that reduced inbreeding and fostered social ties between hunting parties. Each band would be linked to perhaps a half-dozen others in a so-called connubium. Some or all of the bands in a connubium apparently came together from time to time at joint camp-

At present a reconstructed skeleton, this eleven-foot-tall woolly mammoth surely must have been an intimidating creature in the flesh, with its massive bulk and shaggy coat of coarse, reddish-brown hair. In spite of its daunting eight-foot tusks and thick hide, however, the woolly mammoth was a favorite quarry of Clovis hunters.

SANDIA

sites such as the one located at Bull Brook, Massachusetts, which could accommodate as many as 225 people. These gatherings may have been occasions for marriage ceremonies as well as the exchange of gifts such as exotic stones or finished tools and weapons. The meetings may also have served as forums for settling conflicts over territorial hunting rights within the connubium or as opportunities to share meat or other precious resources during times of scarcity.

Perhaps kindred bands also joined in religious ceremonies at these large gatherings. The Clovis people left few clues as to their beliefs. But they apparently harbored faith in an afterlife, as evidenced by a burial site near Wilsall, Montana, where the bodies of two children were interred after being covered with red ocher, a claylike material tinted by iron oxide; this blood-colored pigment was widely employed in burial rites by ancient peoples, who evidently associated it with the symbolic restoration of life. In addition, the bodies were accompanied by more than 100 tools and weapons, including Clovis points and knives—gifts from their kin who believed that the children would have need of the implements as they journeyed to the next world.

Clovis techniques evidently persisted in the woodlands of North America for some time. In the Great Plains, however, the tradition seems

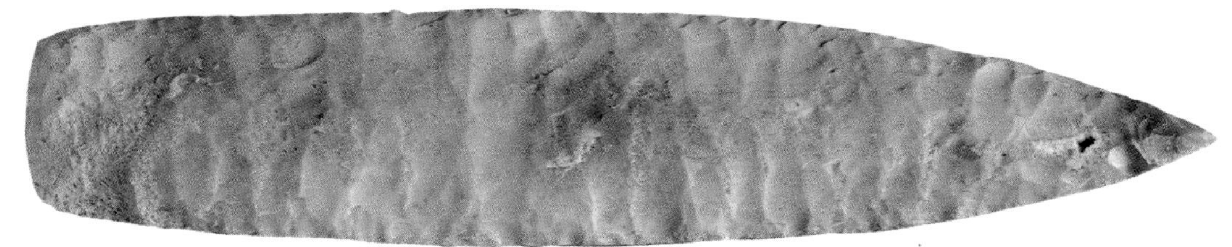
MILNESAND

to have died out around 9000 BC—an event that coincided with the extinction of the mammoth that the Plains hunters had preyed on so assiduously. The success of Clovis bands in bringing down those huge herbivores may have been partly to blame for their disappearance, along with changes in the climate that put added stress on many of the large woolly species that had flourished during the Ice Age. In the absence of the mammoth, the great bison became the hunters' principal target. This formidable species weighed about one ton and supplied virtually everything that the Plains dwellers needed to survive, including not only flesh and marrow but also bones, horns, and teeth for tools, weapons, and orna-

As the population of North America grew and subcultures emerged, the spearpoints that represent these communities took on many forms. Little is known about the people who used the tip labeled Sandia, a name variously applied to a range of simple chipped tools. When hunters of big game developed the Clovis and later Folsom models, they introduced the specialized technique of flaking lengthwise channels in the stone. It is not clear why subsequent communities reverted to the use of unfluted points, such as the Eden and Milnesand.

FOLSOM

ments; hide for clothing, robes, and shelter coverings; and dung for fuel.

With the emphasis on bison-hunting came a new tradition, called the Folsom culture after another site in eastern New Mexico, where a distinct kind of spearpoint—smaller and thinner than the Clovis—was found amid bison bones. Some of these Folsom points turned up in the Great Lakes region, but the tradition was primarily confined to the Plains, where hunters frequenting many of the same campsites visited by their Clovis ancestors adopted the new projectile point along with different strategies for stalking their prey.

EDEN

The Folsom points were both frailer and more delicately crafted than their Clovis counterparts. Ranging in length from approximately three-quarters of an inch to three inches, they were fluted in a wide channel that extended nearly all the way from the base to the tip. Perhaps the longer, wider channel made it possible for the point to fit more firmly into the slotted end of the spear shaft. Yet it also made the point more fragile than the Clovis type—a drawback that may have been of less importance to hunters who were targeting bison rather than mammoths. Consciously or unconsciously, Folsom flint knappers exceeded functional requirements in crafting their lethal spear tips and attained possibly the highest level of stone-chipping artistry achieved by ancient peoples. The edges were delicately chipped, for example, in contrast to the coarser Clovis margins. The key element of the precise fluting was the exertion of pressure rather than percussion—perhaps with the tip of an animal horn—in order to detach additional flakes from the already-thin material without fracturing it.

CLOVIS

Sure-handed Folsom artisans fashioned stone implements for various purposes besides hunting. At camps such as Lindenmeier in northern Colorado, hunters evolved a versatile tool kit. It was composed of thin, sharp knives, scrapers for dressing animal hides, twist drills for piercing wood and bone, and crescent-shaped spokeshaves for straightening and smoothing wooden spear shafts. In order to obtain the obsidian from which many of these tools were fashioned, two different bands that frequented Lindenmeier were required to range far afield. One ventured 350 miles to the northwest, to what is now Yellowstone Park; another traveled just as far to the south, to a quarry in New

Mexico. The two bands evidently rendezvoused occasionally at the Colorado camp, which lay astride the border of their respective territories.

The Folsom people evolved new hunting techniques to take advantage of the bison's powerful herding instinct. They learned to drive large numbers of the animals into box canyons and other natural traps before moving in for the kill. This approach required a joint effort by unprecedented numbers of hunters, perhaps more than one band. The bison's habit of stampeding in unpredictable directions made driving the herds difficult and dangerous, especially on foot. Hunters would work together to plan and execute the entrapment. They might stalk the herd for several days, staying downwind to elude the bison's keen sense of smell. Then, they gradually coaxed the animals toward the trap, using all the tricks in their repertoire. Some hunters may have set fires to divert the animals. Others may have worn bison hides to decoy them in a desired direction.

Bison remained the key to human survival on the Plains for many millennia to come, but hunters there grew more diversified in their tools and techniques. By 8000 BC the Folsom tradition had given way to a half-dozen or so regional cultures lumped together under the name of Plano, whose stone carvers crafted spearpoints of various shapes and sizes that were delicately flaked but lacked any fluting. Possibly the fluting technique simply died out, or perhaps Plano bands discovered that they no longer needed it to secure points that were being directed against prey less formidable than the quarry tracked by their predecessors; the great bison, for example, was disappearing, leaving the field to smaller species of bison, including the creature known today as the buffalo. Whatever their reasons for adopting different spearpoints, Plano peoples expanded on the cooperative tactics of their ancestors by developing new mass-hunting techniques that required even larger parties and the concerted effort of all available members—women and children as well as men.

To the Folsom tactic of trapping and surrounding a bison herd, the Plano added a variant of their own—called the jump-kill—that demanded even more social coordination. In this technique, which was practiced by Indian bands in the Great Plains until long after the Europeans arrived, scores of creatures, sometimes hundreds, were herded into a funnel defined by natural obstacles or by lines of hunters and then stampeded over a cliff or down into a gully. The lead animals, propelled forward by the

A herd of panic-stricken buffalo thunders through the dust. Folsom hunters pursued this modern bison's larger ancestor, using its tough hide–tanned with the animal's own brains–for both shelter and clothing.

frantic followers, plunged over the precipice and were crushed under the weight of subsequent ranks. Hunters then finished off the surviving bison at the upper layers of the pile by aiming their spears for the rib cage and heart.

In addition to using cliffs, Plano hunters devised other means of entrapment. Near present-day Casper, Wyoming, they drove nearly 100 bison into a U-shaped sand dune, blocked the opening, and slaughtered the captives as they tried to climb the loose sandy slopes. In eastern Colorado, they used a formation of slippery, ice-covered snow embankments to the same purpose, bagging around 300 bison over the course of several winters. At the same site, the Plano may have enlisted the aid of a shaman, a medicine man thought to be able to commune with animal spirits. Garbed in a bison hide and mask, the shaman evidently lured the animals toward the hazard before blowing a bone flute to signal the trailing hunters to close the trap.

The archetype of a Plano mass kill, with its careful planning and execution, occurred in late May or early June around 6500 BC near the future site of a town in Colorado named for a frontiersman who would help drive the Indians from the area, Kit Carson. A hunting party of about 150 people—perhaps several bands working together—stalked a big herd of bison as it headed north. Eventually, the bison approached an arroyo, or dry ravine, about twelve feet wide and more than seven feet deep that had long been trod by herds bound for a nearby water hole. Swiftly, the hunters deployed to cut off the escape routes on the east, north, and west. Then with much shouting and brandishing of spears, they triggered the stampede. Bison at the front of the herd rushed down the hill and stumbled into the deep ravine. As they struggled frantically to wrench free, they were trampled to death by their followers, whose fate was soon settled by lethal jabs from hunters standing at the margins of the death pit. In a matter of a few minutes, 193 bison perished.

Dismemberment of the herd proceeded with similar dispatch. Working in teams, the hunters wrestled the carcasses out of the arroyo onto flat ground, rolled them onto their bellies, and slit the hide on their backs with sharp stone knives. Then they pulled the hide down over the flanks to form a mat on which to place the prime tender meat that was located just under the surface, the highly prized steaks from the hump, as well as lesser cuts. Systematically, teams of butchers removed the forelegs and stripped them of meat, followed by the hind legs, pelvis, spinal column, and skull, piling the bones up in that order. As they worked, the hunters

Surrounding a herd of bison on three sides, a band of screaming, waving hunters forces the animals to stampede into a dry gully where those not trampled will be swiftly dispatched with spears. Ancient hunters also used fire to drive unsuspecting herds over cliffs, but they found this method less desirable than the stampede because it singed the valuable hides of the animals.

removed and devoured raw the tasty bison tongue. Butchering was completed quickly, probably in half a day, and then the slower processing of the hides began. About one-fourth of the carcasses were left untouched or only partially butchered, perhaps because they were wedged too tightly in the bottom of the arroyo for convenient handling and were deemed not worth the effort.

The estimated yield from this massacre was prodigious: twenty-eight tons of meat, two tons of edible internal organs, and nearly three tons of fat. Each member of a Plano hunting band, like a later Plains Indian, probably could consume about ten pounds of fresh meat per day. At that generous rate, the harvest would have furnished the 150 participants with fresh meat for more than a month, leaving roughly one-third of the yield to be dried in the sun and packed away for later consumption. Plano peoples devised a means of preserving meat for long periods of time in the form of pemmican—a term derived from the Cree word *pimiy,* which means "fat." This staple consisted of sun-dried meat ground between stones and mixed with hot melted fat. Berries were often added to the blend, which was then packed in storage bags fashioned from animal gut or hide.

Grinding stones—first used by Plano foragers around 7500 BC—were soon adopted by Indians in many locations to grind seeds as well as meat, for people across the continent were resorting by necessity to a more varied diet. It included sundry wild plants as well as small game such as deer and rabbits. This shift reflected a change of far-reaching significance in the North American environment—the dwindling and ultimate disappearance of the big Ice Age mammals. The extinction of the mammoth was just one instance of this mysterious trend. Not long thereafter, mastodons vanished from the forests. By 6000 BC two-thirds of all New World species weighing more than 100 pounds at maturity had become extinct, including the giant beaver and giant ground sloth, and carnivores such as the dire wolf, saber-toothed tiger, and short-faced bear. On the Great Plains, no herbivore heavier than the bison survived the transition. Two venerable grass eaters with links to the Old World—the horse and the camel—were also lost from the American landscape. For the horse, it marked the second such extinction in its remarkable existence. Like the camel, it had first evolved in the New World millions of years earlier and spread to Eurasia over the land bridge during an epoch of glaciation. Its descendants there had then roamed back across Beringia to repopulate the New World after the North American horse died out for the first time. After the second extinction around 9000 BC, more than ten millennia would pass before the horse was reintroduced to the Americas by European explorers. It would be a homecoming of great significance, for the horse was destined to transform the lives of the Plains Indians.

In all likelihood, changes in climate and vegetation in the aftermath of the Ice Age contributed to the demise of many species. As the glaciers retreated far to the north, the middle latitudes of North America became generally drier, with extreme variations in temperature from winter to summer. The sharp contrasts may have upset reproductive cycles or otherwise disturbed the physical systems of mammals attuned to an Ice Age regimen. Furthermore, the trend toward hot, dry summers thinned the herbage. On the Great Plains, grass grew shorter and tougher, meaning that big, lumbering herbivores had to expend more energy to obtain their fill even as dependable watering spots grew scarcer. The advantage went to light-footed grazers with thinner bellies and smaller thirsts.

Fashioned several thousand years ago from buoyant tule reeds that were covered with paint or feathers, these remarkably lifelike duck decoys were uncovered in Lovelock Cave in Nevada. As big game grew scarce, ancient hunters evidently employed lures such as these to attract smaller prey.

But climate alone could not explain why large species that had weathered many earlier episodes of glacial advance and retreat over the eons succumbed during this particular epoch. Almost certainly, human predators who had mastered the art of the big kill played a role in this drama of extinction. Improvements in hunting technology enabled Indians to tap the enormous protein reserves of the great mammals as never before, leading to a growth in the human population, which in turn increased the number of parties preying on those species. According to one estimate, conditions were so favorable for the hunters that a band of 100 Beringians reaching the heart of the continent around 10,000 BC could have doubled in number with every generation. At that rate, they could have reached a population of perhaps a half-million in less than three centuries. If only one in four of them became a hunter and culled prey at the rate of two tons a month, enough large mammals could have been slaughtered in the space of 1,000 years to account for their wholesale extinction—particularly if hunters singled out the vulnerable young members of the herd. Of course, humans faced unpredictable perils of their own, including diseases and storms, which served to limit the population as well as the demands it made on the environment. Nevertheless, the disappearance of more than a few species was probably linked to the proliferation of the human one.

Fortunately for the nomadic Plains dwellers, the buffalo survived and flourished, preserving their basic way of life. Mass kills continued, but they scarcely made a dent in the sprawling herds that monopolized the vast semiarid grasslands. By the time Europeans reached the scene, Indians were killing buffalo at an estimated rate of 2 million a year, yet more than 30 million of the creatures still carpeted the Plains.

In other regions of North America, however, the disappearance of big game had a profound effect on the way Indians lived. Part of the impact could have been spiritual, for the ancient Indians, similar to devout hunters in other times and places, may have sought to commune ritually with the creatures they preyed upon as a means of obtaining their cooperation or seeking their forgiveness. If that were the case, the dwindling away of those species that had so long given generously of their flesh perhaps caused hunting parties to question whether or not they had somehow transgressed—and prompted their descendants to redouble their efforts to honor the spirits of the enduring animals.

In practical terms, the lack of big game forced nomadic bands to seek alternative food sources, and they started to devote more energy to fishing and gathering. By drawing on a broader range of foods, the Indians were less likely to exhaust any one resource, and in most places, they were able to achieve a rough equilibrium with their environment that made it possible for one generation to meet its needs without seriously damaging the prospects of the next. Diversified foraging may well have been an even harder way to subsist than tracking big game, but it led ultimately to a more settled existence for the first Americans. In a few prolific areas such as the Pacific Northwest, with its abundant marine life, groups of Indians would eventually manage to gather enough sustenance from their immediate surroundings to settle down in large, complex communities. Elsewhere, however, the transition to village life required catalysts—seeds that would allow foragers for the first time to raise their own bounty.

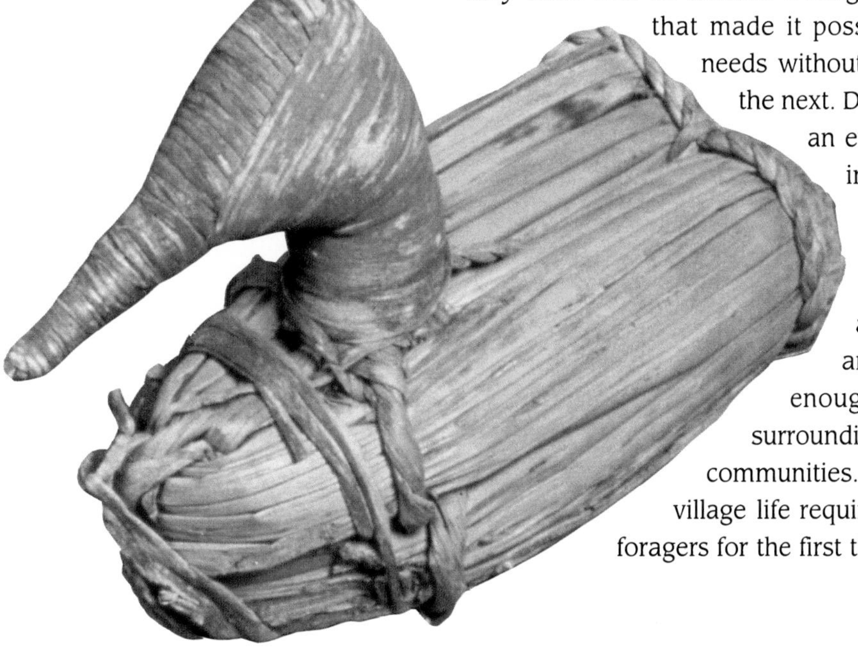

THE GIFT OF CORN

Spaced well apart to best use irrigation water, corn plants dot a Hopi field in Arizona (opposite). These small plants are descended from strains that originated in Mexico—given to humans, according to myths, by beneficent deities, such as the Zapotec god of spring and agriculture. The stone figure below, wearing a corn and feather headdress, was carved around AD 400.

From the arid valleys of the Southwest to woodland clearings along the Atlantic seaboard, Indians lovingly tended fields of corn, a crop that had no rival as a food source. Their names for it were reverential, often meaning "Our Mother" or "Our Life," and in truth, this remarkable member of the grass family supported their world. Legend termed the plant a divine gift to humans, but the story of corn is more complex than that. In Middle America, around 5500 BC, Indians found the way across a great economic divide, leaving behind their total dependence on wild foods and penetrating the mysteries of seed, water, and soil. Among the first crops to be cultivated were squash, avocados, and beans. Corn eluded domestication for perhaps another thousand years, and for a long time, it hardly advanced beyond the version that grew in the wild—an unprepossessing plant with a single bare, inch-long ear holding about fifty small, loosely attached kernels. But around 1500 BC, the novice farmers learned how to cross corn with other wild grasses to create vastly superior hybrids, endowed with multiple ears, protective husks, and cobs that secured row upon row of big, energy-rich kernels. So productive were these hybrids, yielding many hundreds of edible seeds for every one put in the ground, that corn cultivation soon swept across the reaches of North America, lifting whole societies out of a hunter-gatherer past into a more bountiful future.

NURTURING THE SEED

So superb was corn as a food source that although the Indians developed many varieties of the tamed grass over the millennia, they never domesticated another cereal plant. The methods of growing the staple depended on soil, climate, and other factors. Nomadic peoples simply planted the seeds and departed, returning when the corn was high. At the opposite extreme of commitment, some Indians of the Southwest constructed elaborate irrigation systems, such as the one shown below, that made it possible for them to raise two crops a year.

With the advent of more sophisticated farming techniques, men and women assumed distinct roles in the production of corn. Men tended to all aspects of working the fields, from clearing the land to harvesting the crop. Women took charge of preparing and cooking the corn. Some of the ears were treated as a delicacy and eaten at once—boiled, roasted, or raw. But most of the crop was stored in a dark place to await later consumption. As needs arose, the corn kernels were ground into meal or flour for bread, gruel, hominy, and other daily fare.

The Hohokam people of the Southwest needed only simple wooden tools for corn cultivation: a digging stick (right) to prepare a hole in which a few seeds were placed; a spur hoe to remove weeds that would compete with the corn for moisture; and a rake to keep the soil loose around the plants.

Living along the Gila and Salt rivers from AD 300 to 1300, the Hohokam dug a network of canals to carry river water to their vast cornfields that yielded crops in July and November.

In the Southwest, a stone hand tool called a mano was used with a base called a metate (below) to grind corn kernels after they had been stripped from the cob and pounded to remove the husks.

A row of corn plants, incised into red sandstone near the Grand Canyon during ancient times, honors the source of human well-being.

A Hopi kachina doll, carved from a cottonwood root and symbolically painted, represents the spotted corn spirit, Avatshoya, which fosters the growth of corn.

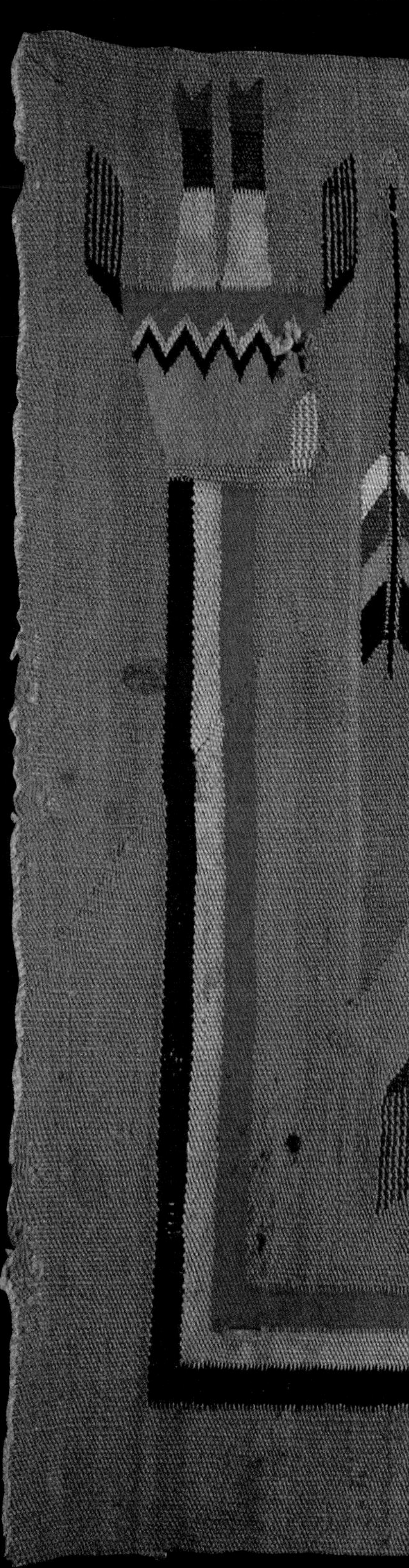

THE SANCTIFIED PLANT

For the Indian peoples, corn was more than nourishment. It was the underpinning of their very existence, and they sensed divine forces at work in the yearly transformation of seed to heavy-laden stalk. Those forces were honored in myriad ways. Rituals dramatized and invoked them; stories explained them; religious imagery depicted the earth-sprung stalks; and the spirit of the plant was given physical form by sacred objects such as the Corn Mother made by the Hopi—a fetish consisting of a perfect ear, adorned with feathers and bound with string. All these expressions of faith and homage were intended to keep the bonds between the natural and spirit worlds strong: Only if the two were fully conjoined would the soil prove fertile, the rains come when needed, and the ears ripen to feed humankind for another year.

Flanked by two supernatural beings and surrounded by an image of the rainbow, a sacred corn plant stands at the center of this nineteenth-century Navajo blanket.

RITES OF CULTIVATION

Rituals involving corn were woven into the fabric of Indian life. The Osage protected infants by rubbing them with cornmeal. Corn figured in the name-giving ceremonies of many tribes. The Choctaw made marriage arrangements during a corn festival. And the Hopi greeted each day by scattering cornmeal toward the rising sun.

Most important of all were ceremonies that enlisted the help of the spirits during the various phases of cultivation. In the Southwest, such rites still lie at the heart of communal life. Dances, songs, and other activities—a few public, most secret—sanctify the seed, summon the rain, celebrate the appearance of the stalks, and at the joyful climax of the yearly miracle, give thanks for the harvest.

Spruce branches carried and worn during a corn dance at a Tewa Pueblo in New Mexico signify everlasting life. Below, a young Tewa girl holds two ears at one of the tribal dances that centered on corn.

2

PEOPLE OF THE DESERT

Dwarfed by towers of sun-burnished sandstone, an Indian of the Hopi tribe surveys the jumbled landscape where at one time his Anasazi ancestors thrived. The Anasazi made the most of the parched desert terrain of the American Southwest.

Descendants of the ancient Americans who settled the Southwest and constructed the sunbaked pueblos say that their earliest ancestors emerged from a dark underworld and roamed the earth restlessly until they learned by the grace of the gods to cultivate the soil and glean wealth and wisdom from the land.

"Deep in the lowermost womb," Zuni legend attests, "the seed of men and creatures took shape, multiplying in kind and increasing until the space was overfilled." Assisted by merciful spirits, the Zuni ancestors ascended to the world of daylight and trod the young earth, wandering and warring with other tribes until they happened upon a land of many houses. "We are the people of the seed," the proud settlers of that place assured them, "born your elder brothers and led by the gods!"

"Not so," replied the wanderers, who had carried seed with them from the underworld and considered themselves uniquely blessed. To prove their powers, the nomads gathered seven seeds of different colors in a gourd, breathed prayers into them, and planted them beneath the stars. Seeing tender sprouts emerge, the settlers praised the feat but remarked that the seedlings as yet lacked the capacity to bear fruit: "Come, let us work together to perfect what you have begun."

Accordingly, the settlers chose seven holy maidens and invited the wanderers to appoint a sacred young man of their own to join them in a ceremony. Moved by the songs of their elders, the youngsters danced through the night beside the seedlings. "As time went on, the matron of the dance led the youth and the first maiden apart and had them grasp, one on either side, the first plant, and dance around it, gently drawing it up." The young man repeated the coaxing gesture with each maiden in turn until all seven plants had grown as tall as the dancers, with joints showing where the youngsters had touched the stalks. As day dawned, husks burst forth at the joints, and through the new leaves gleamed the miraculous kernels of many colors, shrouded in soft silks.

Marveling at the kernels, the wanderers saw that the seed people were indeed led by the gods. "Truly, you are our older brothers," they acknowledged, "and we will cherish your maidens and the fruit of their flesh." Happily, they remained with their hosts, to wander no longer. "Thus, many houses were built together near the plains where the corn plants first grew abundantly."

Through such legends and in the rituals that are performed during the growing season, the Zuni and other Pueblo peoples of the Southwest have long celebrated the gift of corn, which helped transform the lot of their ancestors from a life of ceaseless roaming in pursuit of wild plants and animals to a settled existence in which succeeding generations built on the accomplishments of their predecessors and complex cultures evolved. As the legend suggests, that process began when nomadic bands came in contact with strangers who had fathomed the secrets of agriculture. The original "seed people" of the New World were Indians who settled in the temperate valleys of Middle America as the glaciers were retreating toward the Arctic and who eventually developed domestic strains of corn and other crops. Borne northward over a period of time by travelers, the agricultural lore of the Middle Americans slowly took hold among the hunter-gatherers of the Southwest and altered the character of life in the region.

Extending from the northern reaches of present-day Mexico through Arizona and New Mexico to southernmost Utah and Colorado, the prehistoric Southwest was bordered by an unyielding desert to the west and vast plains of grass to the east. While far from being a land of plenty, this diverse tableau of mountains, mesas, ravines, and river valleys had enough water to support crops in many areas, an abundance of sunshine, and inhabitants who were ready to work the soil if only because other sources of livelihood were limited.

In time, the cultivation of plants had a profound impact on the Southwest, fostering the development of sizable communities of multistory dwellings accommodating artisans of great skill. But nowhere in the Southwest did agriculture eliminate the people's need or knack for foraging. As inhabitants of a land of generous vistas and demanding soil, the early Southwesterners kept their

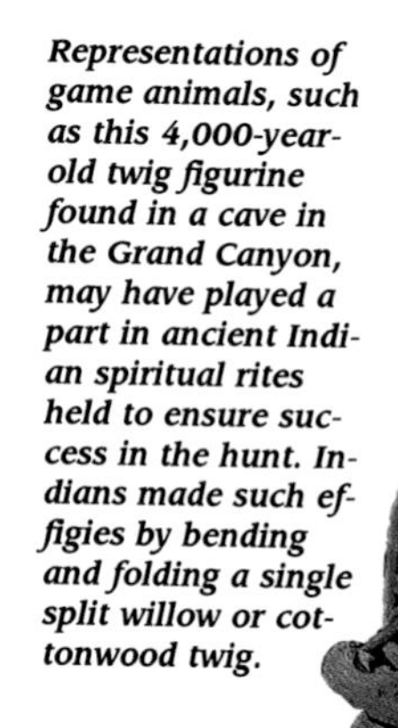

Representations of game animals, such as this 4,000-year-old twig figurine found in a cave in the Grand Canyon, may have played a part in ancient Indian spiritual rites held to ensure success in the hunt. Indians made such effigies by bending and folding a single split willow or cottonwood twig.

eyes trained on the horizon, watching for passing game or sprouting growth that would supplement the harvest and sustain the community through blight or drought. And during periods of deprivation, settlers were prepared to abandon their homesteads and journey in search of a better place. The nomadic tradition ran deep, and centuries of patient planting and harvesting could not expunge it.

The enduring southwestern practice of foraging—a search that overlooked no serviceable plant or animal, however spindly or scrawny—became established around 6000 BC, following the extinction of the great Ice Age mammals. Unlike their predecessors, the new generation of hunter-gatherers in the region could not count on a regular supply of big game as a source of sustenance. The largest of quarry remaining on the continent were buffalo, and they were concentrated in the Great Plains. To be sure, the Southwest was by no means barren of prey. Graced with a somewhat wetter climate than that of today, its grasslands harbored large herds of antelope. In addition, deer, elk, and bighorn sheep haunted the forested uplands. But such fleet-footed herbivores were not easily culled in large numbers. As a result, hunting bands remained small and highly mobile. And no party could afford to overlook lesser quarry such as rabbits, which were snared in nets woven of plant fiber. Little of the carcass went to waste. Strips of rabbit pelts were tied and woven onto a yucca-fiber base to form the blankets and cloaks that, along with hides from larger game, protected those who roamed the high country through cool days and chilly nights.

For the nomads of the Southwest, the onset of winter was a time to hunker down. Many bands sought refuge in caves and rock shelters gouged out of the sides of steep canyons over the ages by running water. The best accommodation was offered by niches that were deep enough to keep occupants and their stores dry and faced south so that their mouths caught the sun for a few hours each day. There, groups of Indians settled in during late fall, carefully storing away what provisions they had been able to collect on their journeys.

As the days shortened and snow dusted the mountain peaks, hunters made frequent forays to stalk deer and elk moving down from the heights for the winter; like their ancestors, these hunters relied on the whiplike action of atlatls to propel their spears, although the stone points on their projectiles were now smaller in keeping with the size of the quarry. Meanwhile, gatherers prepared for the hard months ahead by culling the edible parts of dozens of plants, including juniper berries, walnuts, and

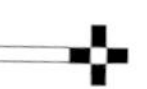

Ancient hunters and gatherers adapted as best they could to the forbidding terrain of the Southwest, at times taking shelter in caves etched into the faces of precipitous cliffs. The cave at far left, located in northeastern Arizona, housed the Anasazi settlement of Betatakin in the thirteenth century.

cactus fruit such as prickly pear. Among the most nutritious of the prizes they sought were the nuts of the piñon tree, which often lured harvesters far afield since bumper crops in any particular area occurred one year in seven at best. As winter progressed and the more perishable items were depleted, the cave dwellers relied largely on wild grains such as Indian rice grass. Relatively easy to transport and store, the grains were ground into meal with stone utensils.

In a sense, these winter camps served as the seedbeds of cultural development in the Southwest. Working with wild grains prepared later generations of Indians to make use of corn and other domesticated plants. Left behind in some caves were twig figurines of animals that may have been used by hunters to charm the spirits of wild creatures before stalking them, setting a precedent for the splendid rituals that later galvanized entire Pueblos. And cliffside alcoves of the sort occupied by the hunter-gatherers ultimately became the sites of fortresslike villages of masonry, which melded architecture with the landscape in a way that has seldom if ever been surpassed.

As yet, the Indians of the Southwest had little occasion to refine such communal skills, for they seldom stayed in one place very long. By early spring, the stores of grain and meat in their caves were exhausted, consumed by the hungry inhabitants. With few possessions to weigh them down, the people dispersed and roamed the countryside again in small bands, scavenging for roots and berries or pursuing sparse game during the lean season that preceded the burst of new growth. Eventually, the region's settlers would have the means to withstand such intervals of scarcity without shifting their base, but not before they learned to put the sun to work in irrigated fields and build year-round structures to shelter the harvest and the settlers who depended on it.

Beginning about 1500 BC, the inhabitants of the region moved slowly and tentatively from a nomadic to a settled existence. The domestic corn first introduced to the Southwest from Middle America around this time was a primitive type with small cobs and served as only a minor supplement to the traditional diet of meat and wild plants. At higher altitudes, the soil was moist enough to nourish the seeds to maturity without irrigation. Migratory bands could plant corn near their winter camps in the spring and return in the fall to harvest a limited crop. Over the centuries, however, the Southwesterners acquired or developed more productive strains of corn that could flourish in the drier soil at lower elevations, provided that enough water was channeled to the roots during critical growth stages such as the tasseling period of early summer. The development of simple forms of irrigation, along with other strategies such as planting different strains at various times and places to guard against the loss of an entire crop, increased the yield at harvesttime and strengthened communal bonds, encouraging people to settle near the fields and send out hunting and gathering parties as required. In addition to corn, the early Indian settlers planted beans—rich in protein—and squash, prized both for its tasty pith and for its rind, which could be fashioned into dippers and containers.

Working the land was not necessarily any easier or healthier than the ancient nomadic regime had been. Indeed, during peak seasons the early farmers of the Southwest, wielding wooden implements, probably had to labor two or three times as many hours as they would have if they had been subsisting by means of hunting and gathering, and the resulting diet was no more nutritious. The combined pressures of increasing population and dwindling wild resources, however, left the region's inhabitants little choice but to devote more energy to agriculture. And gradually, Indians working the fields devised ways of maximizing the harvest and preserving it for longer periods of time, thus affording growing communities a modicum of security.

Crucial to this process was the appearance around AD 200 of ceramic containers that protected stored food against pests and moisture. In the craft of pottery as in horticulture, the settlers of the region may have been inspired to some degree by traders or migrants from Middle America, where artisans had been fashioning fine pots for centuries. Yet little outside prompting was required: The Southwest had plenty of clay soil, and the trick of mixing it with water and a tempering agent such as sand, molding the tractable mass to the desired shape, and baking the vessel by the heat of a fire was one that could and did occur to many resourceful peoples independently. However pottery originated in the Southwest, the crafting of earthenware vessels helped tie the Indians to the land. In contrast to light wicker baskets, pots that were filled with food not only encouraged people to stay in one place by extending the useful life of the harvest but discouraged movement as well by dint of their sheer weight and fragility. Anchored down by their stores, settlers concentrated on amassing a surplus that would not only see the community through lean times but also allow residents to devote a good deal of time to skilled tasks such as molding clay pots.

The urge to preserve and exploit the harvest spurred another skill at

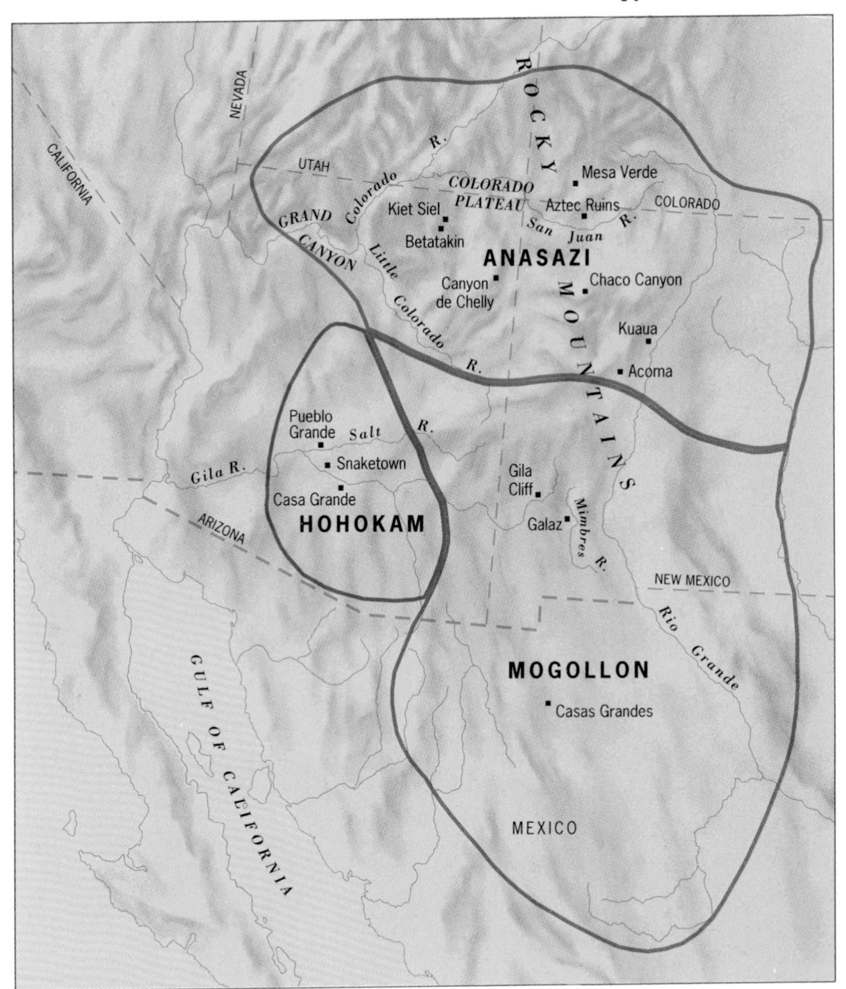

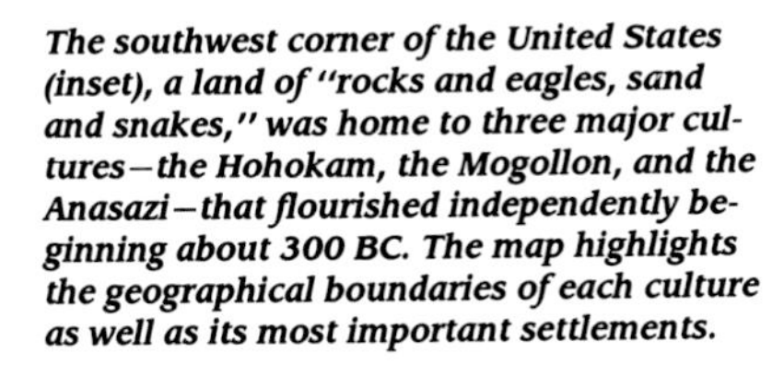
The southwest corner of the United States (inset), a land of "rocks and eagles, sand and snakes," was home to three major cultures—the Hohokam, the Mogollon, and the Anasazi—that flourished independently beginning about 300 BC. The map highlights the geographical boundaries of each culture as well as its most important settlements.

which the Indians of the Southwest came to excel—the building of durable communal shelters. The first permanent dwellings in the region were pit houses, whose floors were set a few feet below the surface of the earth; timber beams supported walls that were made of branches or thatch covered with mud or adobe (dried mud tempered with straw to make it less brittle). Entered by means of a narrow opening in the roof or wall, these modest structures offered room enough for only a family and its scant possessions, leaving little protected space for storing food or preparing it. As the reliance on agriculture increased, residents built aboveground shelters near the pit houses to be used as granaries. Eventually, some of the villagers found it more efficient to live side by side with their neighbors in multichambered, aboveground structures featuring distinct areas for storage and for chores such as grinding—complexes that the Spaniards later dubbed pueblos. Easily expanded by building new apartments beside or on top of existing ones, the pueblos reflected the close bonds between neighbors forged by centuries of seeding, reaping, and milling. There, families tended the harvest together and joined in religious ceremonies designed to ensure the survival of the settlement.

Even in the best of times, most villagers in the Southwest led an austere life. In warm weather, they wore little—sandals on their feet and a breechcloth or apron about the waist. Footwear was indispensable, for in addition to their agricultural tasks, men and women often roamed far in pursuit of game, wild plants, and wood for building and burning. Some communities exhausted local resources over time and had to relocate, while others guarded against that fate by dispatching a segment of the population to distant parts when their numbers increased. Not many people lived beyond the age of forty, and their burials were generally simple affairs; the deceased journeyed to the next world with little more than a worn pair of sandals, perhaps, or a few pieces of pottery that had been

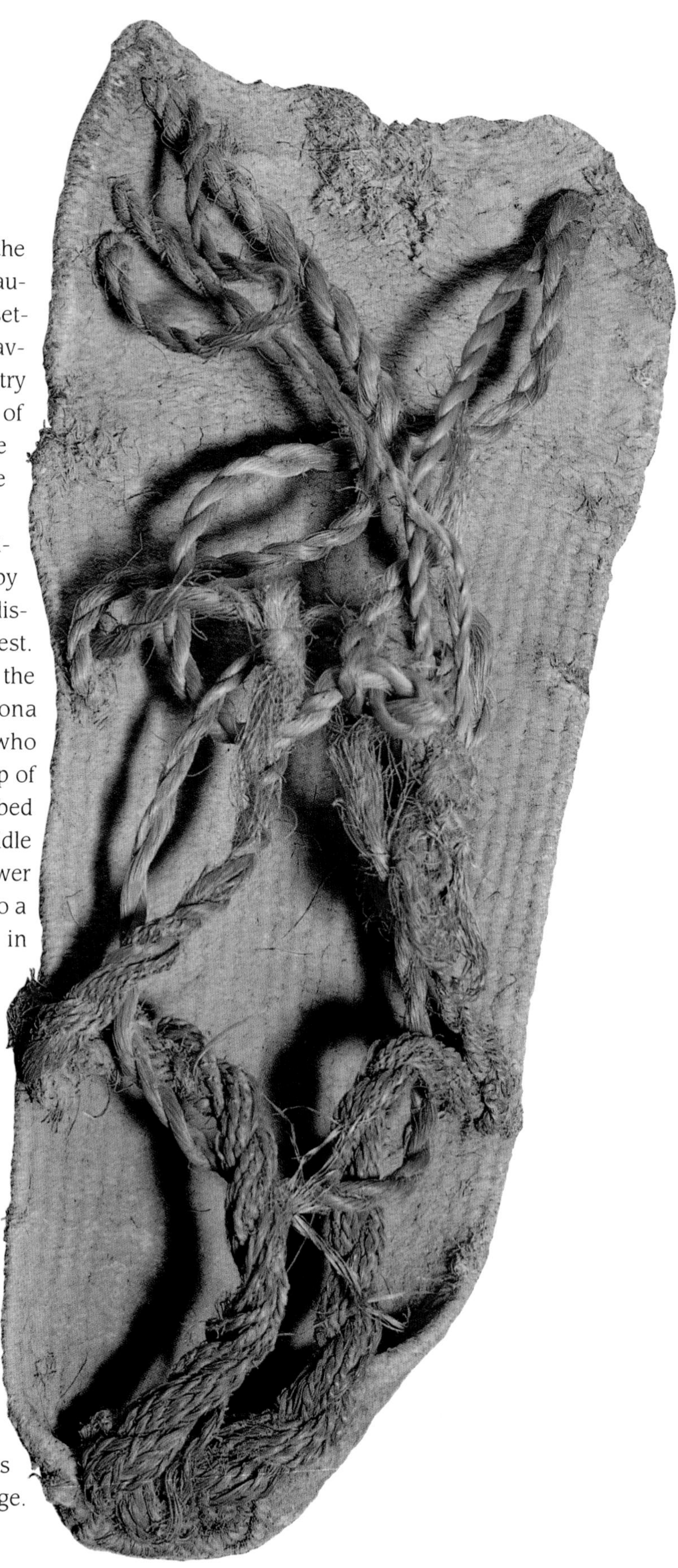

placed in the grave. Yet the earth rewarded the Indians for their constancy. The deathless beauty of the land—of red cliffs burnished by the setting sun and forested mountains rising to heaven from the desert plain—inspired their artistry and devotion, and the miraculous greening of fields in the dry days of spring endowed the community with hopes that transcended the fate of a single individual or family.

As communities that were practicing similar customs proliferated within areas defined by rivers, mountain ranges, or canyon walls, distinct cultures developed across the Southwest. Three principal groups emerged. Inhabiting the south-central portion of present-day Arizona were the Hohokam, a disciplined people who built large riverside communities with the help of ambitious irrigation projects and who absorbed many cultural traits from the settlers of Middle America. The rugged mountains along the lower Arizona-New Mexico border lent their name to a second culture—the Mogollon, who lived in smaller settlements and made independent advances in such skills as ceramics even as they maintained economic ties with other groups. Populating the mesa tops, cliffsides, and canyon bottoms across the region's northern tier were the Anasazi, the architects of imposing structures that endure to this day. Smaller groups inhabited other localities, and the lines between the various cultures were constantly blurred by migration and by trade. Underneath the broad distinctions, however, lay a common tradition of the Southwest—that of people who lived resourcefully in a land of marginal resources and laid such sturdy foundations that neither drought, disease, nor subjugation at the hands of the Europeans could eradicate their heritage.

Winding down from the mountains to the east, two nourishing waterways known today as the Gila and the Salt rivers converged in a cactus-studded plain and surged westward to join the cloudy, silt-laden torrent the Spaniards christened the Colorado. During recent times, the Gila and the Salt have been dammed to meet the needs of Phoenix, Arizona, and its environs and do little to relieve the harsh prospects of the Sonoran Desert. But at one time, they ran unimpeded, and their banks were shaded by willows and cottonwoods. Fish darted amid the rushes, waterfowl rode the current, and deer crept down in the evenings to browse and slake their thirst. Drawn by this bounty, foragers frequented the area, seeking shelter in jacals—huts of bent poles covered with brush and mud.

With the emergence of agriculture, permanent settlements developed near the riverbanks as farmers exploited the silt deposited by floodwaters to nourish seedlings. The simple huts gave way to sturdier rectangular pit houses, and by AD 300, the hamlets were taking on the aspect of organized communities. Most villages boasted a larger building amid the smaller ones, all encircling a central plaza. Covering an area of up to 100 square yards, this big house most likely served as a communal meeting place. Aside from harvesting corn, beans, and squash, villagers ventured into the desert to cull wild growth such as the fruit of the towering saguaro cactus, whose sweet buds ripened in early summer and could be eaten fresh, dried for later consumption, or pressed to yield a syrup that might then be fermented.

Beginning around AD 500, those who lived along the two rivers and their tributaries—a people later dubbed the Hohokam, a Pima Indian word signifying things that are gone or used up—underwent a cultural transformation that set them apart from other village dwellers in the Southwest. In some respects, their customs came to resemble those of the great Middle American civilizations to their south, whose practices included intensive agriculture, astronomical observations to mark the seasons and determine planting times, ritual bloodletting to appease the gods, and the building of ball courts and platforms or pyramids for civic and sacramental purposes.

The Hohokam may have absorbed Middle American influences indirectly through trade links that went back centuries. Or perhaps they were converted to new ways by emissaries from the south—much as the Pueblo Indians were later proselytized by the Spaniards. However the customs were acquired, by the seventh century, some of the Hohokam had aban-

Native yucca plants supplied the Anasazi with woody fibers that they wove into sturdy sandals, shown here life-size. The sole's inner and outer surfaces displayed different patterns. Knotting on the underside may have furnished traction on wet surfaces.

doned traditional burial rites and were cremating their dead—a practice that was followed by part of the population in Middle America but one seldom encountered among the Mogollon or Anasazi. The ashes were interred along with evocative clay figurines of humans and animals much like those crafted by artisans to the south. Around the same time, laborers at some villages began to excavate the earth to create elliptical arenas resembling ball courts; figurines that appear to represent ball players were later found at Hohokam sites along with balls that may have been used during the competitions. Perhaps spectators gathered around the courts to view matches similar to those staged in Mayan palace complexes, where players reenacting a mythic contest were required to advance the ball without using their hands and the losers sometimes paid with their lives. No evidence has surfaced to indicate human sacrifice among the Hohokam people, but small stone vessels left at cremation sites may have held offerings of human blood that priests obtained from the living with sharp bone implements called scarifiers—another custom that was prevalent in Middle America.

Near the ball courts in Hohokam villages rose low earthen platform mounds that served a ceremonial function. At one major settlement containing about 1,000 inhabitants known as Snaketown—situated south of present-day Phoenix—a ring of eight mounds circled a central plaza flanked to the west by a large ball court and to the east by a smaller one. Facing each other at the north and south ends of the plaza were two groups of houses, each with a prominent building in its midst that may have been the meeting place of a clan that shared civic responsibilities with its opposite number. Apparently, this plaza was the hub of an energetic community possessed of dramatic rituals that commanded the respect of the populace and encouraged the collective discipline necessary for ambitious public works.

Preeminent among the accomplishments of the Hohokam was a remarkable network of irrigation canals that eventually extended in excess of 500 miles and increased the amount of arable land by tens of thousands of acres. Some of the conduits were more than fifty feet wide. By one estimate, the main canal system of the Salt River valley would have taken a crew of 100 men thirty-five years of uninterrupted labor to excavate—a figure that excludes the effort required to dig feeder ditches from the canals to the fields and to maintain the system. More likely, the work was performed seasonally over the course of many generations by teams who either toiled willingly or were pressed into service. The irrigation

Some 900 years ago, Hohokam athletes may have matched their skills on this ball court at Pueblo Grande, situated in present-day Phoenix, Arizona. The ancient ball (inset), fashioned from a gummy extract of the guayule plant, is one of the few surviving examples of its kind.

network appears to have been part of a coherent development scheme. Villages with ball courts emerged along the canals at even intervals of about three miles. More than 1,000 years before the same area became the site of sprawling suburban tracts and farms, the Hohokam engineered an expansion that lasted for centuries without exhausting the fragile reserves of water and soil.

As settlements proliferated under the impetus of irrigation, villagers began to live together in closer quarters. In contrast to the loose clusters of pit houses erected earlier, townspeople by the twelfth century were congregating in snug compounds containing rows of contiguous adobe rooms with unexcavated floors; some of the buildings rose two or three stories in pueblo fashion. Large towns contained up to twenty of these rectangular compounds, each surrounded by walls; projecting from the roofs of the buildings were eaves of timber that shielded residents engaged in outdoor chores from the fierce sun.

The walled compounds probably housed families related by blood or marriage, but a strong civic bond linked the various kinship groups, as evidenced by imposing platform mounds that dominated the villages.

Atop these big platforms—some of which measured more than 100 yards long and 50 yards wide—stood small temples that took up only a portion of the available space. No longer were the mounds associated with ball courts; older ceremonial centers containing ball courts, such as Snaketown, had been abandoned. Perhaps a version of the ball game, or some other communal ritual, was now performed atop the platform. Plainly, the villagers attached great importance to the temple mounds, for during the thirteenth century, residents of high status began to build houses there alongside the temples. Reflecting the privileged position of the platform dwellers, their homes were filled with goods that bore witness to far-reaching trade and fine handiwork.

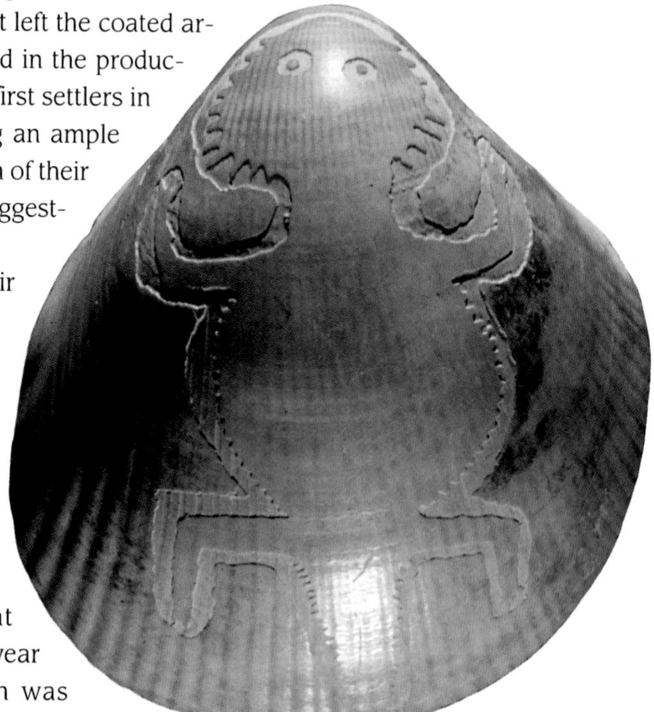

The Hohokam Indians, perhaps the first people to master the art of etching, created this image of a horned toad in a cockleshell imported from the California coast. In a process that was developed about AD 1100, the artisan applied an acid, such as the fermented juice from the saguaro cactus, to the shell to produce the design in relief.

Aside from exchanging goods with merchants from Middle America and with their Anasazi and Mogollon neighbors, the Hohokam traded articles with the Indian peoples who lived along the Pacific Ocean and the Gulf of California. From those coasts came shells that Hohokam artists etched with intricate designs by coating a portion of the surface with a protective veneer—most likely pitch—and soaking the shell in fermented cactus juice or some other corrosive solution that left the coated area raised in relief. The Hohokam also specialized in the production of cotton fabrics. Apparently, they were the first settlers in the Southwest to grow cotton—a crop requiring an ample supply of water and a long growing season. Much of their weaving was done on the platform mounds, suggesting that they held the craft in high esteem.

Some of the local Hohokam artists left their designs on the nearby landscape. In the desert surrounding the irrigated settlements, where groups of villagers went to forage for wild plants and game, revealing pictures were scratched or painted on rocks. A number of the images represented hunting scenes and may have served as good-luck charms; in some cases, the hunters themselves were portrayed wielding bows and arrows, an innovation in weaponry that spread throughout the Southwest around the year 500. Another popular Hohokam motif, which was found on pottery as well as on rocks, depicted a long line of dancers holding hands—a fitting emblem for this tight-knit society.

The Hohokam built one of their loftiest monuments about the year

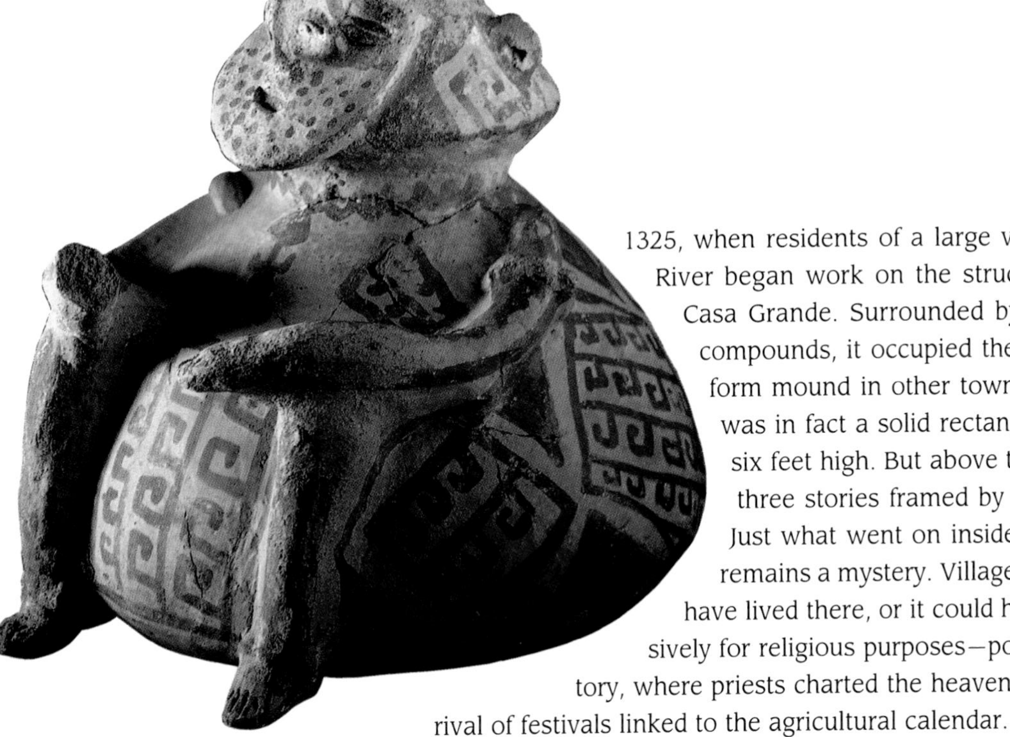

1325, when residents of a large village below the Gila River began work on the structure later known as Casa Grande. Surrounded by a cluster of walled compounds, it occupied the position of the platform mound in other towns, and its foundation was in fact a solid rectangular mound of earth six feet high. But above that ground floor rose three stories framed by thick walls of adobe. Just what went on inside this imposing tower remains a mystery. Villagers of importance may have lived there, or it could have been used exclusively for religious purposes—possibly as an observatory, where priests charted the heavens and foretold the arrival of festivals linked to the agricultural calendar.

In the Snaketown settlement, the Hohokam used human effigy jars like the one above, probably for ceremonial purposes. The sharp angle formed by the neck of the vessel, the geometric design, and the red-on-buff paint all typify Hohokam pottery produced between the years 900 and 1150.

Casa Grande signified one of the final constructive feats of a culture that had dominated the area for more than a millennium. Beginning in the second half of the fourteenth century, many Hohokam villages were abandoned—a fate that befell numerous settlements around the Southwest during the period. A prolonged regionwide drought, punctuated by sporadic downpours, may have stripped fields of topsoil and silted up the canals. Whatever the nature of the crisis, the Hohokam people had at last encountered circumstances to which they could not adapt, and they either set out in search of new homes or reverted to a nomadic existence, leaving behind a fertile record of accomplishment in a thirsty land.

The waters exploited so successfully by the Hohokam issued from a mountainous region that was home to a distinct culture—the Mogollon—named after one of several clusters of peaks that rose along the Arizona-New Mexico border. From that high divide, the Gila and Salt rivers snaked westward toward the Gulf of California, while to the east smaller streams and washes descended to the Rio Grande and thence to the Gulf of Mexico. At higher elevations, this steep watershed offered only narrow pockets of land suitable for farming. Hamlets sprouted up there nonetheless—perhaps because early settlers feared assault and flocked to remote places for defensive reasons—but most of the communities remained small, compared to Hohokam villages, and the inhabitants depended to a greater extent on hunting and gathering.

Faced with a colder climate than that experienced by settlers in the lowlands to the west, these early mountain dwellers excavated pits up to four feet deep for their dwellings and fashioned ramps that led down to the floor from the entrance. Firepits near the base of each ramp were stoked with timber felled with stone axes in the surrounding forests of spruce, fir, and pine. Air flowing through the entryways fed the fires, while smoke holes in the roofs vented the fumes and sustained the draft. Insulated by the earth and by a thick layer of adobe lining the walls aboveground, these pit houses kept their occupants warm through the long winters that gripped the high country.

Below the peaks, where the terrain descended gently and the hills were dotted with scrubby juniper, oak, and piñon, valleys opened that offered Mogollon settlers room to expand. One such area of opportunity existed along the lower reaches of the Mimbres River, in southwestern New Mexico. The first hamlets there evolved about AD 500 and consisted of small groups of round pit houses. Families probably carried out simple religious ceremonies within the walls and often buried their dead beneath

the floors, so that over time the pit houses became associated with the spirit world. Villagers later adopted a rectangular plan for their houses but honored tradition by gathering in large, round pit houses called great kivas. One such meeting place at a site called Galaz was more than forty feet wide, spacious enough to hold most if not all of the community's sixty or so inhabitants, who sat around a central hearth and one or more carefully plastered holes filled with fine white sand. Pueblo Indians who inherited kiva rituals from the Mogollon and the Anasazi referred to such holes as *sipapus*—symbolic passageways to the underworld from which the spirits of the ancestors emerged.

By AD 1000 the inhabitants of the Mimbres Valley had developed a crude masonry technique—laying river stones in a mortar of mud or adobe—and were erecting aboveground structures. This innovation, possibly spurred by contact with the architecturally advanced Anasazi, conferred several advantages. Excavating a pit house was an arduous task for people who had no metal tools and relied instead on wooden implements. And while most occupants lined the floors as well as the walls of their pit houses with adobe, the structures were far from impervious to vermin and moisture; when the supporting timbers rotted, pit houses had to be razed. Aboveground masonry lasted far longer, kept the inhabitants and their stores relatively dry, and allowed residents to expand their homes by constructing contiguous rooms—an option pit house dwellers had to forgo because their walls would collapse unless buttressed by earth. Soon, villagers along the Mimbres were congregating in complexes of a dozen or more rooms, where resources could be pooled and tasks such as grinding could be carried out collectively.

Cooperation was important outside the home as well. Although the Mimbres Valley did not lend itself to large-scale irrigation projects like those carried out by the Hohokam, simpler forms of water control extended the arable land beyond the flood plain and up into the hills on either side of the river. Villagers constructed a series of check dams at intervals of twenty to forty feet along hillside streams to catch the runoff and collect silt, forming terraces for farming. The labor involved was modest, but organization of some kind was surely required to distribute lots fairly and prevent disputes from arising. No evidence exists of an elite class that imposed its will on laborers and grew wealthy by their toil. In all likelihood, the equitable use of water and soil was an article of faith among the villagers, backed by leaders with religious authority and bolstered by rituals that reminded individuals of the debt they owed to the community

The semisubterranean walls of a Mogollon pit house provided its residents with natural insulation from the winter cold and summer extremes—up to 100 degrees Fahrenheit by day, and near-freezing by night. Saplings radiated from a central support to form a conical roof that was daubed with a thick layer of mud. The Mogollon often built their pit houses on defensible, well-drained mesa tops and ridges that gave farmers a good view of their fields below.

and to the gods who sustained it. As settlements expanded, their inhabitants ceased to meet as a unit in great kivas and gathered instead in smaller kivas attached to room blocks. Yet villagewide ceremonies persisted, most likely in the open plazas between the room blocks. In such plazas today, members of various clans or religious societies emerge from their kivas on holidays to join in dances that unite the Pueblo.

At its height in the eleventh century, the Mimbres Valley subculture comprised a dozen or so major villages with a total population of perhaps 3,000. The tilling of irrigated fields combined with resourceful foraging yielded enough of a surplus to make it possible for some of the residents to devote much if not all of their time to crafts—in particular the production of painted pots, at which Mimbres artisans excelled. Many of their finest works were put to household use, then interred as grave offerings after first being ritually pierced and placed over the head of the deceased. These vessels were punctured, or "killed," to enable the spirits of the figures decorating the bowl to accompany the soul of the dead person on its way to the underworld.

Like their counterparts elsewhere in the Southwest, Mimbres potters worked without a wheel. Instead, they molded clay into coils and wound

When a Mimbres Indian died, family members frequently interred the body beneath their house in the position shown above. The head was covered with an inverted pottery bowl.

them to the desired width and height, then smoothed and shaped the walls of the vessel with their fingers and scraped them with a stone or gourd (Hohokam artisans used a different finishing technique that left the surface dimpled). To decorate their works—an increasingly common practice as ceramics became prized as trade items and grave goods—potters applied a slip of pure clay to create a smooth surface that would hold paint. Mimbres artisans made slips from a white clay known as kaolin, to which dark paint was applied using brushes fashioned of yucca fiber that had been chewed until soft. Pots were fired in a makeshift kiln composed of large fragments of discarded pottery stacked under and around the fresh creations.

With a steady hand, Mimbres potters painted their works with intricate geometric patterns, some of which resembled natural features such as mountains, clouds, lightning, flowers, or feathers; designs were sometimes divided into four quadrants, perhaps reflecting a world-view that invested the cardinal points—north, south, east, and west—with cosmic significance. Other southwestern cultures employed similar motifs, but Mimbres potters distinguished a number of their works by combining the characteristic geometric motifs with marvelous depictions of animals, hu-

Mimbres potters used simple colors—white combined with black or red—but they portrayed with verve the creatures of the desert world: the birds, animals, and insects that shared their environment.

When the sun crowns 443-foot-high Fajada Butte (above) and climbs to its apex at noon on June 21, the summer solstice, a single shard of light bisects the nine-ring sun symbol (inset, right) for a period of eighteen minutes.

REVELATIONS FROM THE SUN

To the people who inhabited the ancient Southwest, the movements of celestial bodies signified the journeys of gods. Being able to predict the perceived movement of the sun in its seasonal rounds meant knowing when animals would migrate, when the time for planting was at hand, and when the season for life-giving rain was imminent. Observers, probably shamans or priests, studied the moon, stars, and planets to discern universal patterns of movement and incorporated the knowledge into religious rites and mythology; one ancient Indian ritual was performed to ensure that the sun on the shortest day of the year would not disappear forever. Avid astronomers, the Anasazi constructed the unique sun calendar illustrated below. Three stone slabs placed against the face of a butte in Chaco Canyon, New Mexico, funneled the sun's rays into daggers of sunlight that announced the new seasons to those skilled in their interpretation. The device marked solar time for some 700 years, until in the late 1980s, erosion shifted the massive stones.

Engineered with precise geometry, the Anasazi sun calendar divided the year into four quarters by marking the first day of each season with a distinctive pattern of sunlight shining upon spirals (below) that were inscribed on the side of Fajada Butte. The stone slabs that lean against the butte were oriented by the Indians to the changing height of the midday sun during the year.

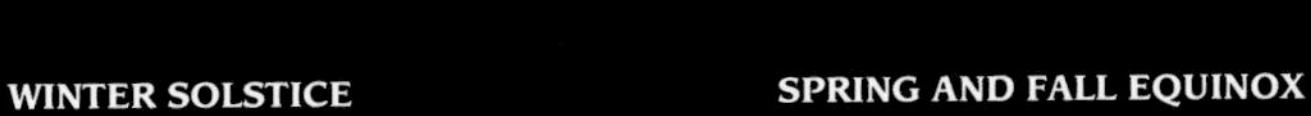

WINTER SOLSTICE

SPRING AND FALL EQUINOX

SUMMER SOLSTICE

mans, and hybrids. As these works reveal, the inhabitants of the region, despite their increasing reliance on agriculture, maintained an avid interest in the creatures around them and felt a certain kinship with the species they stalked. One painted bowl shows a line of hunters with birdlike beaks holding hands as they pursue a wild turkey—a scene that may represent a dance in which the performers donned masks to capture the spirit of their quarry before the actual hunt.

As population increased in the Mimbres Valley, local resources were being depleted. The riverbanks, once lined with cottonwoods and alders, were all but denuded of trees, and deer and other sizable prey grew scarce. When the climate turned drier around AD 1150 and agricultural production lagged, the once-prosperous villages came under severe stress. Those residents who weathered the crisis were apparently absorbed by an expansive culture to the south, centered at the Mexican town of Casas Grandes, a commercial hub with trade ties reaching deep into Middle America. Signaling the change in authority, some inhabitants of the Mimbres Valley began to practice cremation while others adhered to the traditional form of burial. A few of those buried were found without skulls—victims, perhaps, of a new and harsh regime.

Elsewhere in the Mogollon domain—in higher places less vulnerable to drought and outside influences—settlements maintained their cultural identity and persevered for another century or two. And at a few isolated sites such as the Gila Cliff Dwellings, new villages of masonry were built in alcoves of rock. But those efforts could not compare either in scale or in workmanship with the construction projects undertaken farther north by the master builders of the Southwest: the industrious Anasazi.

For a people who would erect the largest dwellings found anywhere north of Mexico before the industrial revolution, the Anasazi began their sedentary existence in humble fashion. Occupying a land of countless canyons and ravines whose cliffs were riddled with inviting cavities, they continued to rely on such natural shelters long after the practice of agriculture tied them to one spot for much of the year. As late as AD 500, many settlers across a broad expanse extending from the upper Rio Grande to northeastern Arizona still lived in cliffside alcoves similar to those that housed their ancestors in the winter. These early Anasazi stored their harvested crops in pits that were plastered with clay and covered with stones, and worked and slept beneath eaves of overhanging rock. Nevertheless, signs of a new way of living were in evidence. Here and there, the cliff dwellers sought further protection from the elements in jacals or in shallow pit houses. After a period of time, they left the protection of the cliffsides and built homes along the canyon bottoms or on mesa tops. Whichever setting they chose, they were able to take advantage of both habitats, culling timber and nuts from the forested heights, and fish, fowl, and berries from the valley floors.

The resource that was the most influential in shaping the Anasazi culture, however, was the sandstone the Indians either found in piles at the base of some cliffs or quarried there. This sedimentary rock occurred in layers, so that chunks found or extracted along the cliffs were naturally flat at the top and bottom; stoneworkers had only to pare them down lengthwise to produce handy building blocks. By about the year 800, Anasazi artisans were amassing these sandstone blocks in order to erect houses of masonry. At first, the walls they raised were thin and fairly crude, with stones of various dimensions set randomly in mud mortar. But before long, Anasazi masons were laying stones of uniform shape in neat patterns that were both pleasing to the eye and structurally sound. Frequently two courses deep, these sturdy walls supported stout rafters and adobe roofs. Ladders protruded through narrow hatches in the ceilings that doubled as smoke holes. The hatches also afforded inhabitants easy access to their own rooftop, which provided a tidy workspace during fair weather. Originally, the Anasazi room blocks were single story, but improvements in masonry techniques meant that the ground walls could support the weight of two or more floors. By AD 1000 the first multistory pueblos appeared. Typically, their stories rose in stairstep fashion so that residents could continue to make use of the rooftops.

Like Mogollon villagers, Anasazi pueblo dwellers gathered in circular kivas that resembled the pit houses occupied by their ancestors except that the kivas were deeper and incorporated special features such as benches. Residents entered the kiva at plaza level by means of a ladder that descended through a hatch into a cavernous space lighted by fire. Seated around a sipapu symbolizing the passage from the underworld, their ghostly shadows flickering against the high wall, kiva-goers may have sung songs, told tales, or meditated quietly on their origins and destiny.

This female effigy sculpted in Casas Grandes, Mexico, more than 500 years ago possibly displays the clothing, hairstyle, and facial paint worn by the settlement's inhabitants at that time. Casas Grandes, a trading center, may have absorbed the last members of the Mimbres culture.

Sunlight streaming into the depths of an Anasazi kiva in Utah illuminates the sipapu, a small hole in the kiva floor that is believed to be a gateway to and from the spirit world. Known to Southwestern Indians as "center of centers, navel of navels," the kiva symbolizes the mythic realm from which humans emerged. Still used as social and ceremonial meeting chambers, modern kivas house groups of men who discuss community matters, plan harvests, rehearse seasonal rituals, smoke, and pray. The ancient structures (inset, shown without roof) shared common elements. The ventilator, the firepit, and the sipapu formed the room's central axis. Indians descended the tilting ladder facing the rungs; to look down was believed to shorten one's life.

Judging by the customs of Pueblo Indians today, Anasazi kivas may have been reserved for special clans or societies within the village, often exclusively male. Traditionally, women have played an important part in Pueblo society. Indeed, some Pueblos have long been matrilocal, meaning that upon marriage, husbands have gone to live with their wives and their kin. But by and large, the kiva has remained a place for men to commune with one another and with the spirits.

Some Anasazi kivas contained looms, suggesting that in early Pueblo culture as in recent times, men may have served as weavers. Following the lead of the Hohokam, the Anasazi cultivated cotton and wove it into blankets and robes that they wore in cold weather and on ceremonial occasions. Pottery, by contrast, seems to have been women's work—at some sites, women were buried with potter's tools. Among their intricately decorated creations were pipes used to smoke pungent wild tobacco as well as various culinary tools, including jars, cooking vessels, bowls, dippers, and broad mugs with large handles that may have held either water or a kind of gruel prepared from ground corn, which women preserved for long periods by parching it in a basket filled with hot stones or coals. Both sexes wore jewelry, studded with such exotic items as shells from the Gulf of California. And parents in many villages deliberately flattened the backs of their infants' heads by strapping them to hard cradleboards. The motive for this custom was probably aesthetic, but such restraint also allowed caretakers to keep infants close while leaving their hands free for other vital tasks.

Living in clusters of settlements separated by mountains, deserts, and other natural barriers, the Anasazi developed varying customs from place to place and probably spoke more than one dialect, judging by the linguistic diversity of their descendants. But they were linked by ties of trade, craftsmanship, and ceremony. And for a brief interval, scores of far-flung settlements and tens of thousands of people were brought under the control of one great cultural center. This hub evolved in a seemingly unpromising setting—a broad, shallow canyon in northern New Mexico carved by the erratic Chaco River, whose banks sometimes ran dry and remained so for weeks on end. Yet the flat expanse between the cliffs offered an ideal framework for a sophisticated irrigation scheme that channeled runoff from the mesa tops into diversion dams and thence to the low-lying fields through head gates, which maintained a slow, steady flow. In this way, intermittent downpours became a source of prolonged nourishment for the crops. Here, as in the river valleys worked by

Abutting a sheer sandstone cliff, Pueblo Bonito appears below in an artist's rendering as it probably looked at its height in AD 1100. Long a ruin by the time Spaniards dubbed it "beautiful town" in the sixteenth century, the impressive Anasazi settlement (inset) covered two acres in the valley of New Mexico's Chaco River.

the Hohokam, irrigation required a major investment of human energy but yielded a great dividend—a well-fed and well-organized society with the capacity to expand.

By the year 1050, there were more than 5,000 settlers inhabiting Chaco Canyon. Abundant harvests provided sustenance for laborers who built great pueblos and a network of roads under the direction of a central authority. Careful planning marked these construction projects, as illustrated by the symmetrical layout of Pueblo Bonito *(opposite),* a D-shaped, four-story complex of more than 800 rooms that may have been the administrative and ceremonial heart of Chaco culture. One million dressed stones went into the construction of this pueblo alone, whose courtyard was dotted by more than a dozen kivas great and small. Relatively few people were buried near Pueblo Bonito and the eight other multistory complexes erected along similar lines in Chaco Canyon. Perhaps most of the rooms in these great pueblos were used for the storage of crops and trade goods—including a few luxury items from Middle America such as copper bells and tropical birds—all watched over by occupants who distributed the surplus in times of need or as part of some established ritual. Some of those who resided in the pueblos may have been priests, who marked the progress of the religious and agricultural calendar with the help of windows and wall niches situated so as to frame the sun only at solstices or equinoxes.

Near the great pueblos stood modest, single-story room blocks whose occupants may have provided the muscle to haul timber, heft stones, and clear the roads that spoked out in several directions from Chaco Canyon. Intent on laying straight paths, the road builders declined to go around natural obstacles but instead carved steps that rose steeply up cliffsides. When a change of direction was required to reach their goal, they did so at sharp angles. Perhaps such geometric precision had spiritual significance for the Chaco people, but the roads served a practical purpose by linking the Pueblos in the canyon with dozens of outlying settlements. One such outlier, situated about eighty miles northwest of Chaco Canyon along the Animas River, was built on such a grand scale that explorers later dubbed it the Aztec Ruins for its superficial resemblance to Middle American monuments. In fact, this 500-room complex bore all the marks of Chaco workmanship and must have been erected either by colonists from the canyon or by indigenous laborers taking orders from Chaco authorities.

By means of such efforts, the people of the great pueblos were able to propagate a small empire, all of whose roads led to the canyon. But around 1150, scarcely a century after the expansion began, the system began to collapse at its core. In Chaco Canyon, as in the Mimbres Valley to the south, a prolonged dry spell apparently put extra pressure on an area whose resources had already been taxed by a growing population requiring not only food but also fuel and shelter. Obtaining wood for fires and construction, for example, had long been a chore for the residents; during the eleventh century, as many as 100,000 trees had been felled on distant slopes and hauled to the canyon. As the drought wore on and the storerooms of the Pueblos were depleted, the burden of venturing ever farther afield to meet the needs of the community became more than the settlers could bear. Leaders lost their grip, and villagers drifted away, many of them seeking higher ground where water, timber, and other assets were more plentiful. In the aftermath, stiff winds and fitful rains flayed the deserted canyon, leaving a scrubland strewn with the skeletons of great pueblos.

Elsewhere in the region, settlers faced an environmental challenge of an entirely different order. In northern Arizona, near present-day Flagstaff, a people called the Sinagua—who were influenced culturally not only by the Hohokam to their south but also by the Anasazi to their east—found their way of life threatened when a volcano erupted around the year 1065, showering their fields with ash. A second major eruption occurred two years later, and ash may have poured from the vent sporadically for a long time thereafter. Yet the farmers in the belt surrounding the volcanic caldera—known as Sunset Crater—refused to give up on the land without a struggle. They may have derived some long-term benefit from the capacity of ash to serve as a mulch, trapping scarce moisture, but otherwise the eruptions must have complicated the task of working the soil. Nonetheless, the Sinagua held their communities together and maintained a rich spiritual life, as indicated by a splendid burial that took place at a small Pueblo approximately twenty miles east of Flagstaff early in the twelfth century.

The deceased, a man in his late thirties, was decked out in elaborate finery, with a beaded skullcap, ear pendants of turquoise inlaid with shell, and other exquisite charms. Discovered among his grave offerings were scores of ceremonial items, including a set of eight mountain lion claws, perhaps used to summon the spirit of the animal and harness its power. Judging by such talismans, the deceased man was a prominent priest or shaman whose ritual observances had been instrumental in seeing the

For centuries, the people of Acoma had to negotiate the sheer cliffs of their mesa on precarious trails with narrow stone steps and rock toeholds. Before the Spaniards arrived about 1540, the villagers built the Burro Trail (above) to ease the journey to and from the valley below.

A PUEBLO IN THE SKY

Around AD 1300 Anasazi refugees from drought-stricken areas such as Mesa Verde in present-day Colorado trekked south and found a haven up close to the sky—on top of a mesa that rises 357 feet above the surrounding plain. The lofty site, located in modern-day New Mexico, offered the Anasazi a number of advantages: dependable reserves of water and a level plain for the growing of corn, as well as the mesa's sheer cliffs to serve as protection from any potential enemy. "The village was very strong," wrote Castañeda de Najera, a Spanish explorer who happened on the Acoma settlement around 1540. "It was up on a rock out of reach, having steep sides in every direction. It was a very good musket that could throw a ball as high." So secure was the Acoma Pueblo that it has survived to this day, possibly the oldest continuously inhabited village in the United States. Even though they have absorbed the Spanish influence, the people of the community on high cling to the traditions of their ancestors—the traditions of festival and dance, ritual and ceremony.

In this 1904 photograph (left), an Acoma woman fills a clay pot from the reservoir on the mesa's south side. Such pools provided a reliable supply of clear, cold water.

As shown in this photograph taken in the early 1900s, the people of Acoma live in terraced adobe houses some three stories high. Clay required for the construction of these buildings had to be lugged up the cliff from the desert below. Among the dwellings are rectangular kivas for meetings and ceremonies.

Strips of mutton are drying on a line, and corn cobs lie in a heap behind this Acoma father and son in a photograph taken in 1891. Farming and sheep raising are the mainstays of those who live on the seventy-acre mesa. Men and boys tend sheep; everyone participates in the planting and harvesting of crops.

On September 2, 1898, the people of Acoma gathered before the mission church to honor the Pueblo's patron saint, Esteban, in an annual ceremony that still takes place. Legacy of the Spanish conquest of Acoma, the church was built under the direction of a Franciscan missionary between the years 1629 and 1641.

Pueblo through difficult times. No prayers or performances could prolong the fertility of the volcanic plain indefinitely, however. By the thirteenth century, this area too was nearing exhaustion and facing abandonment.

Compounding the difficulty of adapting to changes in the environment was competition among rival groups for scarce resources. Apparently, the Indians of the Southwest were peaceable, avoiding wars that devastated whole villages or claimed a large number of lives. Nonetheless, they were avid hunters who knew how to handle weapons, and during times of stress, some among them may have intimidated others into abandoning their homes or surrendering their stores. Conceivably, a desire to discourage assault was one reason some settlers along the rugged northern and western fringes of the Anasazi domain built sequestered villages in cliffside crevices during the twelfth and thirteenth centuries. The places chosen—known today by such names as Canyon de Chelly and Mesa Verde—tended to be steeper and less accessible than Chaco Canyon. But no evidence has surfaced to bear out the assumption that occupants of the remote cliff houses faced attack or feared it. Perhaps Indians first flocked to such high places simply because their mesa tops caught precious moisture and then built houses in the rock shelters as a way of shielding the buildings and their occupants from rain and snow.

The most extensive cliff dwellings were erected at Mesa Verde, in southwestern Colorado, where forested promontories separated by deep ravines of sandstone towered above the Mancos River and its tributaries. Indians had lived on the fertile mesa tops for centuries, first in pit houses and then in single-story room blocks. But around AD 1200, settlement shifted to the cliffsides, possibly because the villagers needed to use every available acre of mesa top for farming. Using neatly dressed sandstone, masons at Mesa Verde fashioned intricate warrens of as many as 200 rooms, wedged so tightly between the rocky ledges and overhanging arches that distant observers could scarcely distinguish those architectural gems from their setting.

Unlike the pueblos in Chaco Canyon, each cliff dwelling at Mesa Verde followed a markedly different plan dictated by the surroundings. Rooms were low and narrow and stacked as high as four stories where space permitted. Even the slightly built inhabitants—who averaged little more than five feet tall—must have felt cramped in their cells; they passed a good deal of their time crouching around fires, whose smoke soon blackened the cave tops. Here and there, the cliff dwellers erected mysterious rectangular or circular towers, many of them linked by tunnels to great kivas. Despite their superficial resemblance to lookout posts, few of these turrets commanded much of a view. They were probably designed strictly for ritual purposes.

In the end, apparently, a harsh environment rather than hostile intruders drove the Mesa Verdeans from their homes. Notwithstanding their impressive quarters, the cliff dwellers, like most Anasazi villagers, lived a frugal and strenuous life. They acquired few items through trade and relied heavily on hand-me-downs, systematically salvaging building stones and tools from decrepit dwellings and mending broken pots with pitch. Confined as they were to narrow ledges, they of necessity deposited human waste and other refuse close to their homes, a practice that did nothing to improve their chances of survival; approximately half of all children born to the Mesa Verdeans died by the age of four. And as time passed, the farmers who climbed steep stairways that had been hewn out of stone to till the mesa tops reaped diminishing returns. Around 1275, the latest in a devastating cycle of droughts seized the area and held on for more than two decades. Settlers began to move away, sometimes leaving caches of food or clothing behind as if they expected to return. But there was no turning back. By the fourteenth century, Mesa Verde had joined a growing roster of ghost towns across the Southwest.

Evidently, a similar fate befell other groups of cliff dwellings around the same period of time. Haunting testaments to deserted ambitions, those structures left a false impression that the culture that spawned them had been abruptly extinguished, never to be revived. In truth, the abandonment of Mesa Verde, Betatakin, and other hard-pressed communities was offset by the emergence of large pueblos in more favorable locales whose adobe walls were to crumble eventually, leaving little for posterity to admire, but whose occupants were in fact no less accomplished than the cliff dwellers. Many of the exiles from Mesa Verde likely gravitated toward communities that were located along the upper Rio Grande and its larger tributaries—year-round

Stone figurines carved by the Anasazi before AD 1450 may represent some of the earliest examples of kachina, or spirit, dolls. Kachinas personify ancestral spirits and aspects of nature. In present-day Pueblos, Indians continue to honor the 600-year-old kachina tradition by donning spirit masks during their seasonal ceremonies.

waterways that provided the settlers some insurance against a drought.

Typical of the villages that sprouted up in the Rio Grande area in the fifteenth century was Kuaua Pueblo, a sprawling complex of more than 1,000 rooms located some twenty miles north of present-day Albuquerque. Indians displaced by drought flocked to the Pueblo's irrigated fields to raise a variety of crops, including cotton, tobacco, and melons. There, and at other such melting pots, settlers of diverse backgrounds were drawn together by compelling rituals involving kachinas—embodiments of ancestors and of life-sustaining forces such as rain, corn, and creatures of the wild, whose spirits were invoked by costumed dancers on festival days as well as depicted by artists on the walls of kivas and in the form of dolls for the blessing of children.

In some instances, Pueblos were able to grow and prosper without having access to a major river. At the village of Acoma, majestically isolated on a 350-foot-high bluff approximately sixty miles south of the crumbling mansions of Chaco Canyon, residents supplemented the one creek in their vicinity by catching rainwater and runoff from passing storms in rock cisterns and carefully parceling it out to their fields and kitchens. Throughout the Southwest, tight bands of settlers pooled their resources with similar ingenuity and created oases in a parched land. From this triumphant process of adaptation emerged the self-reliant Pueblos that the conquistadors encountered during the sixteenth century. Like their pioneering ancestors, the people of the Pueblos had preserved kernels of hope through unsettled times and planted them in fresh ground, and no amount of coaxing or coercion by the Spanish colonizers could induce them to abandon the ways that had nourished those seeds.

AT HOME ON THE MESAS

In all the vast sweep of America, few landscapes are as dramatic as the Four Corners region of the Southwest. Here, where the present-day states of Utah, Colorado, New Mexico, and Arizona meet at a common point, the high plateau country has been sculpted into a fantastical mix of plunging canyons, flat-topped mesas, vivid-hued sandstone cliffs, and the dark, frozen outpourings of volcanoes. Winters are harsh, and summers regularly torment the land with droughts or violent thunderstorms. Beautiful and challenging, this region long ago became home to one of the most remarkable of Indian peoples—the Anasazi, whose gift for building was worthy of nature's own architecture.

After living a seminomadic life in the area for centuries, the Anasazi embraced farming wholeheartedly around AD 700, gathering in communities and, as they prospered, erecting multistory settlements of sandstone, adobe, and wood. Their most spectacular feats of construction were accomplished from about 1100 to 1300, first in the valley called Chaco Canyon *(right),* then on the tableland of Mesa Verde to the north *(page 87).* Despite a shared culture and extensive trading, the Anasazi remained fragmented—and vulnerable, as events proved. Beginning in the twelfth century, changes in the environment drove them from their ancient homeland to merge with peoples that became the modern Pueblos. The terraced cities were left to crumble in the canyons and on the mesas, lashed by summer rains, swept by moaning winter winds—a haunted memory of greatness.

Once a terraced metropolis that stood at least four stories high and housed perhaps 1,200 people in its 800 rooms, Pueblo Bonito was the greatest of all Anasazi dwellings, dominating the narrow valley of Chaco Canyon in northern New Mexico. The semicircular pueblo was begun around AD 920 and reached its maximum size about 200 years later.

At Chaco Canyon, communal gatherings were held in chambers called great kivas, derived from the circular pit dwellings that housed the Anasazi in their early days. This one was sixty-three feet across and could accommodate several hundred people. It included a perimeter bench, a subterranean entryway, rectangular pits, and massive pillars set in holes in the floor to support the roof.

Aany of the interior spaces at Pueblo Bonito were con-nected by carefully aligned doorways (above) that could be screened with a nat or hide. In ad-lition to its hun-dreds of storage and nabitation rooms, he complex had hirty-seven kivas, nost of them small, ircular chambers right) where men of various clans likely gathered for prayer, song, and talk.

In northeastern Arizona, Anasazi of the Kayenta branch constructed a 155-room dwelling called Kiet Siel under a cliff overhang in Tsegi Canyon about AD 1270. By then, the Anasazi were hard-pressed by drought.

Built on a ledge in a Tsegi side canyon, the 135-room cliff dwelling called Betatakin is dwarfed by the 500-foot-high vault of its rock alcove. Similar to nearby Kiet Siel, the site was abandoned less than two generations after construction. The inhabitants migrated to the Hopi mesas farther south.

Nestled against a cliff in southwestern Utah, a granary fashioned from slabs of sandstone kept rodents and the rain away from the wintertime food supply. This locale, in present-day Zion National Park, lay on the margins of the Anasazi world, far from the primary trade routes and the centers of population.

The so-called White House Ruin, a cliff dwelling named for the white gypsum clay used to coat its upper section, was one of almost 400 Anasazi settlements in the Canyon de Chelly area of Arizona. It housed about forty people.

Situated at the mouth of a cave commanding a spectacular view of Utah's Colorado River basin, this structure, once roofed with poles and brush, served as shelter during bad weather. The Anasazi built many small dwellings in this area between AD 900 and 1250.

Around AD 1200, refugees from the Four Corners area occupied the site known today as Bandelier, in north-central New Mexico, where they adapted their building methods to the soft local rock of compressed volcanic ash. Many dwellings were constructed of rocky fragments that fell from cliffs (left), but the habitations also included rooms that were created by enlarging natural caves or hollows in the cliff face and adding a ladder for access (above).

Maintaining old traditions in their new Bandelier home, the Anasazi built this kiva in a cave 150 feet up the face of a volcanic cliff. Behind it stood a thirty-room masonry dwelling, two stories high in places.

Although they did not begin gathering in large pueblos until after AD 1100, the Anasazi of southwestern Colorado and southeastern Utah were masters of masonry construction, erecting high-walled, almost windowless complexes of cut sandstone blocks. Many of their structures had towers; the ruin above is known as Hovenweep Castle.

Like the Anasaz elsewhere, the Mes Verde people bega seeking the shelte of cliff alcoves abou AD 1200, and the proceeded to buil on a monumenta scale. Biggest o these later dwelling was the one calle Cliff Palace (right) with 200 rooms an 23 kivas. It wa abandoned afte

THE ART OF EVERYDAY OBJECTS

Many centuries ago, the Indians of the Southwest forged a tradition of craftsmanship that elevated the most humble and utilitarian objects to the status of art. These people—the Hohokam, the Mogollon, the Anasazi, and their descendants—began as nomadic hunters and gatherers who crafted baskets as vessels for carrying and storing food and other goods. By 100 BC, they had adopted an agrarian—and more sedentary—lifestyle. Clustered in permanent or semipermanent settlements,the Indians of the Southwest discovered that clay pots, though impractical for a transient existence, were more suitable than baskets for storing and cooking food. The more settled the people became, the more time they had to devote to refining their pottery, and to fashioning jewelry and other decorative items. These crafts assumed a spiritual importance when left as grave offerings at burial and cremation sites. And they represent a rich artistic legacy—a gift from the ancient ones.

The Sikyatki canteen pictured here, named for the Arizona pueblo in which it was found, was crafted around AD 1400. It was slung from a rope that was knotted at the two handles.

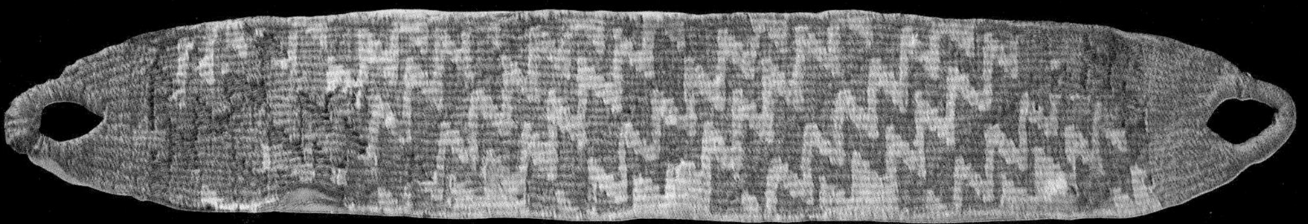

TUMPLINE

THE ESSENTIAL BASKET

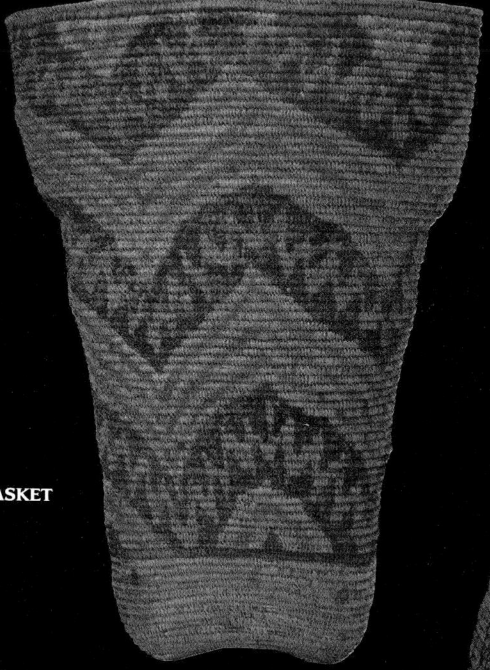

BURDEN BASKET

STORAGE BASKET

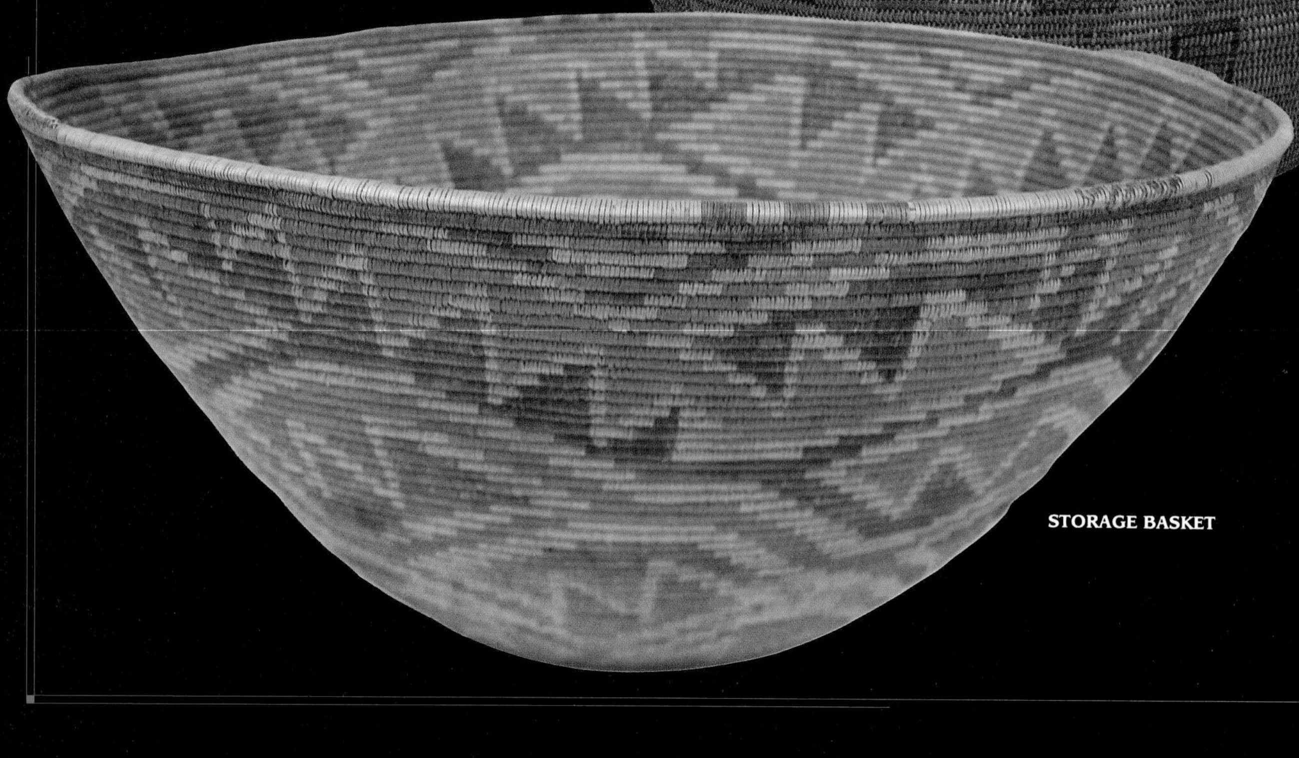

STORAGE BASKET

The ancient Indians of the Southwest designed baskets in different shapes for specific tasks and wove them using a variety of native raw materials, including yucca, bear grass, willow, and squawbush. Burden baskets such as the one at left, used for gathering food, were balanced on the back or the shoulders and supported by woven bands, called tumplines, that went around the forehead. Other baskets, which were tightly woven and coated inside with pitch from the piñon tree (below), held water; Indians boiled their food in such vessels by adding hot stones to the liquid. Two legs strengthened and gave balance to the basket shown at right, which was probably used to transport heavy objects, such as turquoise or shells, for trade.

BIFURCATED BURDEN BASKET

ANASAZI WATER JAR

ADORNING THE BODY

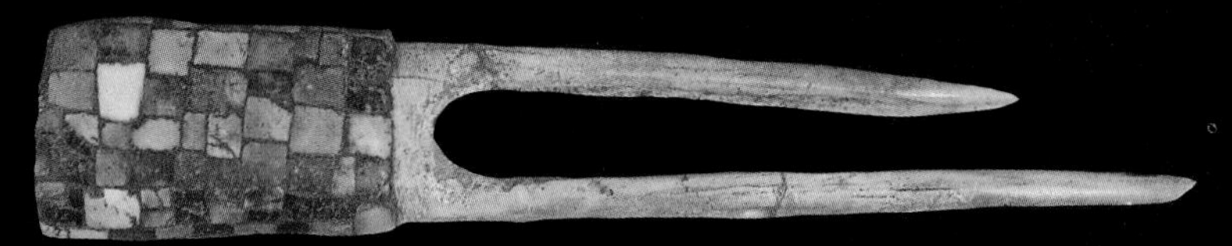

ANASAZI BONE HAIRPIN WITH TURQUOISE OVERLAY

TURQUOISE MOSAIC EARRINGS

As raw material for crafting jewelry, the Indian artisans of the Southwest favored locally mined turquoise, which they considered sacred, and shells imported from the Gulf of California. They fashioned delicate bracelets, necklaces, pendants, and rings from the shells of oysters, clams, and abalone. They strung tiny conus shells together to make "tinklers," or noisemakers worn during ceremonial dances. And using mesquite gum and piñon pitch, they wed stone to shell to create exquisite mosaic pieces.

SHELL AND TURQUOISE SUNBURST EARRINGS

ANASAZI TURQUOISE NECKLACE

MIMBRES SHELL NECKLACE

HOHOKAM GREEN SLATE BIRD PENDANT

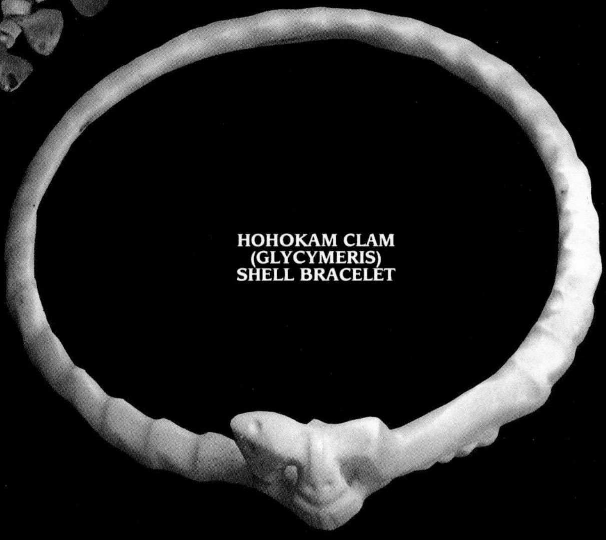

HOHOKAM CLAM (GLYCYMERIS) SHELL BRACELET

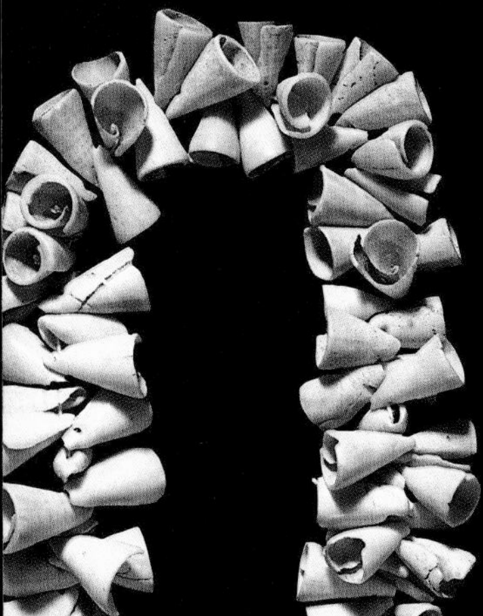

HOHOKAM CONUS SHELL NOISEMAKER

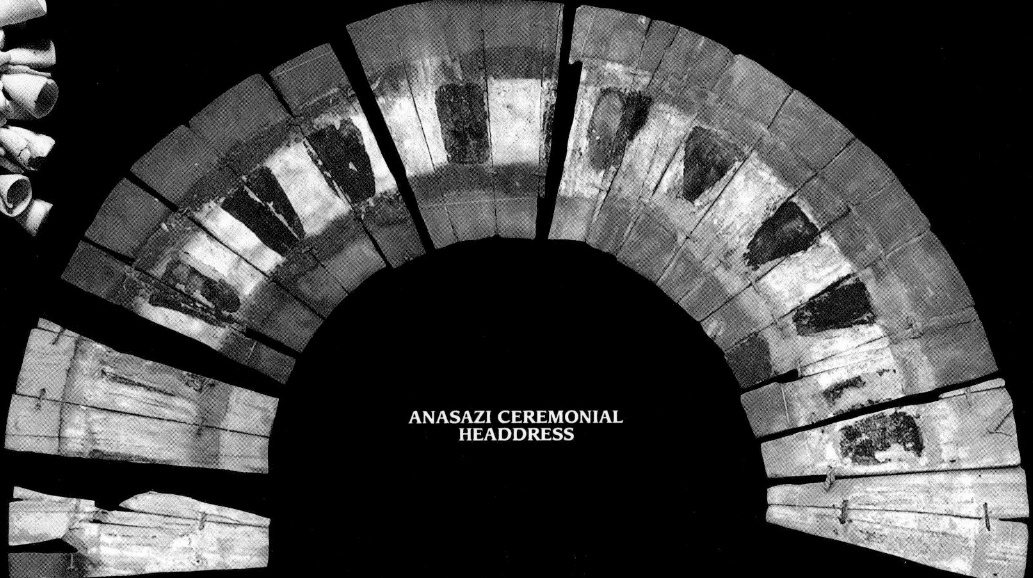

ANASAZI CEREMONIAL HEADDRESS

ANASAZI PITCHER

The first potters of the Southwest learned to coil ropes of clay to form vessels and to harden them in a fire. From then on, ceramic containers assumed many of the functions previously served by baskets. The first pots were crude forms of unadorned gray clay, but soon Indian artisans were crafting shapely bowls and jars and painting them in sophisticated patterns adapted from basket designs. Decoration and color varied from culture to culture; black, white, red, and brown predominated.

SAINT JOHNS WATER JAR

MOGOLLON BLACK-ON-RED BOWL

HOHOKAM RED-ON-BUFF JAR

SOCORRO WATER JAR

LADLE FROM CHACO CANYON, NEW MEXICO

3

THE MOUND BUILDERS

Monument of a vanished people, a huge pyramid-shaped earthen mound built by Indians of the Mississippian culture more than seven centuries ago rises above the surrounding forest at Moundville, Alabama. The building on top represents the divine ruler's dwelling, which crowned some ceremonial mounds in ancient times.

More than 1,000 years ago, near the confluence of two great rivers known today as the Missouri and the Mississippi, a teeming settlement arose in the depths of the woodlands. More populous by far than any of the ancient villages of the Southwest, this remarkable civic hub, called Cahokia, drew wealth from as far away as the Gulf Coast. Up the Mississippi in dugout canoes paddled Indians bearing bundles of precious goods coveted by Cahokia's artisans and their masters—alligator teeth, barracuda and shark jaws, pink conch and ornate scallop shells. The traders who carried such prizes to that destination must have eagerly anticipated their arrival, and not merely in the hope of receiving valued articles in exchange. For to reach Cahokia was to feast one's eyes on fabulous sights.

The travelers' first distant glimpse of the goal might be less than inspiring—a pall of smoke from the smudge fires that helped keep down the mosquitoes infesting the swampy bottom lands. But when paddlers left the broad river and swung their canoes into the creek that led to Cahokia, they could see welcome clusters of loaf-shaped pole-and-thatch dwellings and hear the invigorating chock-chock of axes and the insistent yapping of dogs. Along the banks of the creek lay fields of corn, with beans, squash, gourd, and sunflowers mixed in tangled profusion around the ragged margins of cultivation. Farmers toiled there, bending low over their flint hoes. Farther on, the clumps of huts became more frequent. Artisans squatted on the packed earth, with cutting tools of chipped stone or fire-hardened cane in their hands, fashioning stone axes or polishing shells to serve as cups and bowls. Others tied copper or bone hooks to long fishing setlines, or worked with stone gouges over the oak logs they were sculpting into canoes. Here and there, variously shaped mounds rose above the fields. Some were small, conical affairs, but others were large, truncated pyramids, with temples on their flat tops.

The greatest of these pyramids rose at Cahokia's vast central plaza, which was bounded on one side by the creek where traders landed and unloaded their goods and on the other three sides by a heavy wooden palisade. So immense at the base that a strong bowman could scarcely shoot an arrow from one end to the other, the earthen pyramid rose in steps to four broad terraces, the highest of which overshadowed all but the tallest trees. Atop the terraces, plumes of smoke issued from shrines where guardians tended sacred fires night and day.

Ordinarily, the plaza at the foot of the pyramid would be filled with hunters, farmers, and artisans of every description, eager to exchange goods with the newly arrived traders. But at times of festivity or mourning, commerce would give way to ceremony. When spring brought new life to the fields or autumn yielded its harvest, the plaza would become the site of hectic footraces or ritual dances, carried out to the beat of hollow log drums and gourd rattles. And on those occasions when death claimed the life of a great chief or high priest, the body would be conducted up the ramp of the pyramid to a funerary temple by a solemn file of celebrants—among them relatives or retainers of the deceased who might soon be dispatched to join their lord in the next life.

When it reached its apogee around 1100, Cahokia was home to at least 10,000 people, making it the leading metropolis of the richest and most complex culture north of Mexico. Much of its wealth and splendor was made possible by a generous environment. In comparison with the Indians of the Southwest, the inhabitants of the eastern woodlands profited by a more benign climate, lusher plant and animal resources, and a wider network of waterways that facilitated long-distance trade. Those assets nourished the growth of large settlements led by powerful chiefs, who patronized artists of great skill and took many of their exquisite creations with them to the grave.

The culture of which Cahokia was a part—known as the Mississippian for the river along which many of its prominent villages were located—was not the first to take root in the eastern woodlands. It had two proud predecessors, the Adena and the Hopewell, both centered on the Ohio River drainage system and characterized like the Mississippian by an assortment of villages whose residents communicated through trade, pursued a mixed farming and foraging economy, and built mounds as places of interment and worship. In time, the mounds—some of them prodigious efforts rivaling the monuments of the Maya and other advanced peoples of Middle America—proliferated by the thousands. They bordered every major waterway of the continental heartland and stretched eastward through the tangled forests to what is now New York,

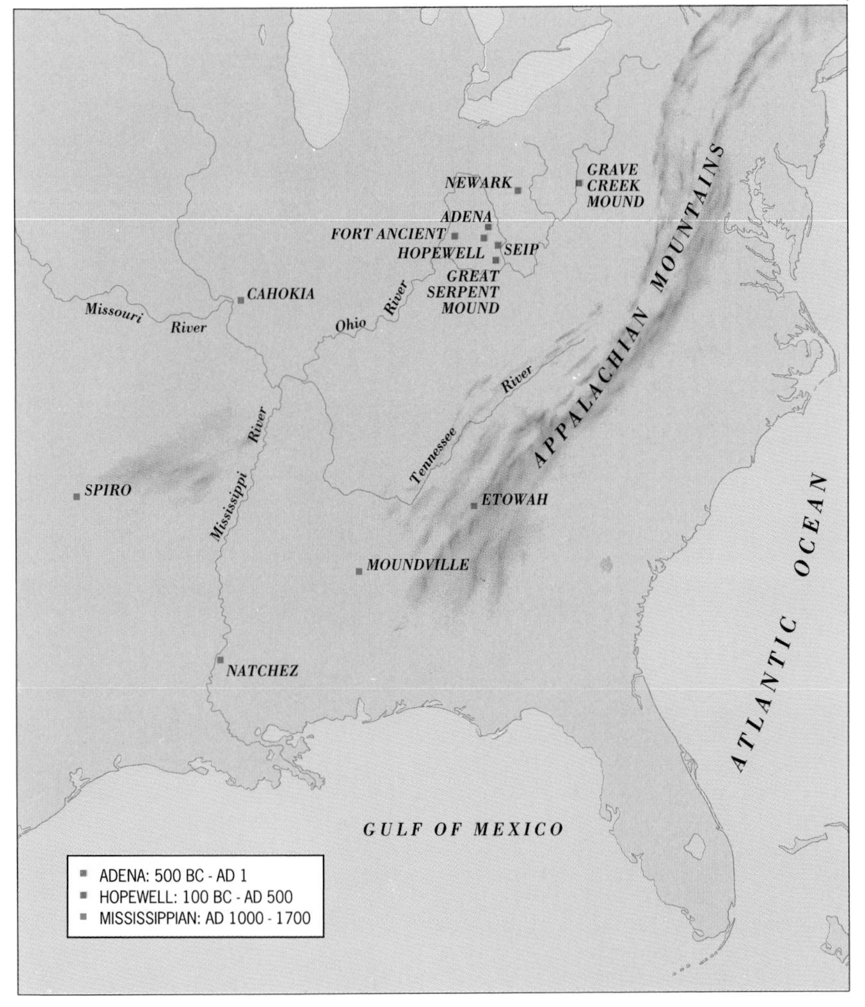

The map above locates some of the principal settlements of the three successive Indian cultures that flourished in eastern North America during ancient times. The Adena people built their villages and mounds mostly in present-day southern Ohio, with settlements in the neighboring states. The Hopewell, who were concentrated in Ohio and Illinois, spread across much of the Midwest. The third and latest culture, the Mississippian, was far more extensive than the others, reaching from the Mississippi Valley southeast to Georgia and Florida, north to Wisconsin, and west into Arkansas.

southward along rich alluvial valleys to Florida and the Gulf Coast, and westward into portions of the Great Plains. In many locations, as at Cahokia, the cones and pyramids were enclosed within extensive palisades and earthworks, some of which served their creators as forts. In a few spots, however, the mound builders allowed their imaginations to roam freely, molding low earthen ridges in the shape of giant animals.

The antecedents of these energetic mound builders were nomadic hunter-gatherers who entered the eastern woodlands toward the end of the Ice Age. Early on, the upper tier of the region—above present-day Tennessee and North Carolina—was covered by pine forests that gave way to tundra close to the margins of the glaciers. But as the ice retreated toward the Arctic, the deciduous forest and dense vegetation of the Southeast spread northward—along with squirrels, rabbits, opossums, woodchucks, raccoons, turkeys, deer, bear, and other creatures adapted to that habitat. The Indians of the woodlands became keen students of this diverse animal world, learning to track dozens of species. Equally attentive to wild plants, they supplemented their kills by harvesting an assortment of seeds, berries, and nuts. They fished the clear lakes, streams, and rivers for bass, bowfin, and catfish, using bone hooks and harpoons. And in the dextrous fashion of the ancient Indians throughout America, they supported their foraging activities by fashioning stone tools and weapons—knives, projectile points, scrapers, axes, gouges, mortars, and pestles.

The early forest dwellers moved in small bands from camp to camp, taking shelter in tents or flimsy huts and timing their migrations to coincide with seasonal variations in plant and animal resources. From about 4000 BC onward, however, the pressure of increasing population gradually restricted this nomadic pattern. Foraging bands were forced to confine their range and rely to a greater extent on storage techniques and trade contacts with neighboring peoples.

In southeastern coastal areas, Indians camped for much if not all of the year close to inlets and on barrier islands whose protected waters harbored an abundance of shellfish and waterfowl, among other creatures. Judging by the large middens, or deposits, of discarded shells left behind by those foragers, certain sites were visited by sizable bands for extended periods of time, year after year. At a mini-

The bottle shown at left, modeled in the simple shape of a mother and child, was made in Cahokia, the largest Mississippian community, depicted in the reconstruction below. The city included high mounds topped by homes for the ruling class (right) in addition to scores of temple mounds. To the left of the huge central plaza were thatch-roofed dwellings for the thousands of ordinary inhabitants. The towering pyramid in the background, the largest prehistoric structure in North America, may have covered as many as twenty-three acres—more than the Great Pyramid of Egypt.

mum, Indians probably lived near such middens from spring to early fall. Some of the bands buried their dead beneath heaps of shells, while others laid down floors of crushed shell or clay and built shelters over them. They did not have to depend exclusively on the water for their livelihood. Deer and other game could be hunted at the margins of the forests that backed the marshlands and estuaries, and in the fall the woods were carpeted with acorns and hickory nuts. As trade ties expanded up and down the coastal rivers, bands who frequented the islands and tidewater areas discovered that the larger or more alluring shells they collected were prized as utensils, ornaments, or ceremonial items by the people who were settling down inland.

The adoption of a rudimentary horticulture helped make it possible for the woodland Indians to live in one place for most of the year without suffering seasonal shortages of food. Their garden tending, which was conducted in clearings and along riverbanks, consisted originally of little more than reseeding indigenous plants—sunflower, pigweed, marsh elder, goosefoot, knotweed, maygrass—and returning to harvest the crop several months later. Nevertheless, this was incentive enough for the establishment of hamlets whose populations evolved new skills and increasingly intricate customs.

In fertile locations such as the rich bottom lands of present-day southern Illinois, perhaps 100 to 150 people came together and put up a half-dozen structures of wood, plaited branches, and clay. To conserve and cook their food, they crafted vessels of soapstone or clay, and employed handstones and grinding slabs to prepare the seeds and nuts. At a site known as Indian Knoll in what is now western Kentucky, settled around 2000 BC, hearths were dug into the hard-packed clay floors, and the same fires that cooked the food served to warm the huts against the blasts of winter. Here as elsewhere, subsistence was enlivened by trade and artistry—prized possessions included ornaments fashioned from copper mined in the Great Lakes area and cups of conch shell obtained from the Gulf of Mexico or the Atlantic Ocean. When villagers died, articles that denoted their roles or status were placed in their graves. Men were buried with axes and fishhooks, women with pestles and nut-cracking stones. The bodies of high-ranking individuals were often lavished with extra grave offerings.

In a number of villages, the Indians saw fit to bury the dead on the summits of hills, closer to the vault of the sky. North of the Ohio River, in the Great Lakes region, villagers began around 1500 BC to inter their dead on the tops of kames—mounds of gravel that had been deposited by glacial melt. A similar impulse caused people at far-flung sites to pile earth or gravel higher on existing hills, or to create mounds in the lowlands. Some of these earthworks were used for purposes other than burials. At Poverty Point in modern Louisiana, for example, Indians inhabiting the Mississippi flood plain built several imposing mounds of a ceremonial nature around 1400 BC. The largest was nearly seventy feet high and bordered by a series of artificial ridges, atop which villagers made their homes. The considerable effort that went into such mound building indicated that Indian settlements across the region were becoming increasingly stable and well organized, with leaders who could orchestrate the

A 2,000-year-old pipe, carved by an Adena craftsman, shows a dwarf wearing decorated britches and enormous spool earrings. Strong native tobacco, smoked during rituals, was packed in a bowl between the feet; the mouthpiece was in the top of the figurine's head.

efforts of large numbers of people and communal rituals that bound one generation to the next.

Such were the roots of the Adena culture that arose around 1000 BC and survived for more than a millenium. The first woodland tradition to link villages across a wide area through trade and ceremony, its focus was the central Ohio Valley, within a 300-mile radius of present-day Chillicothe and an estate called Adena, site of a burial mound characteristic of the culture. Although the Adena lived in permanent settlements and grew crops, they relied primarily on hunting and gathering for subsistence. Like the hunters of the Southwest, they practiced rituals designed to summon the spirits of the animals they stalked and to seek their cooperation or forgiveness. Adena shamans wore antler headdresses, and a few may have even knocked out their upper front teeth so that they could hold wolf jaws in their mouths when they appeared in ceremonies and when they were committed to the grave. Communing with nature in this fashion was probably regarded both as a religious obligation and as a practical necessity if the creatures of the woodlands were to surrender flesh, bone, and sinew to the grateful hunters.

The Adena lived in village clusters of up to a dozen dwellings that most likely housed related families. They framed their simple round houses with rings of posts, between which they wove walls of flexible material such as cane. The roof was constructed of tough matting or thatch, and in the center of the floor lay a firepit for cooking and warmth; outside, there was sometimes a hole gouged from rock for grinding seeds and nuts with wooden pestles. Most of the huts accommodated only five or six people, but some were larger and may have been communal dwellings housing up to forty.

The rhythm of daily life began with the rising sun. Carrying wooden spears that were tipped with points made of chipped stone, the hunters were out at first light, gliding through the forest in search of deer, elk, or smaller prey. Others worked the streams and lakes for catfish, box turtle,

tle, and freshwater mussels. Meanwhile, gatherers scavenged for walnuts, acorns, and chestnuts, along with wild plants such as pawpaw and raspberry.

For a steadier food supply, villagers equipped themselves with wooden hoes that were fitted with blades of chert or shell—or with a cruder digging tool wrought of an elk's shoulder bone—and cleared rough spaces at the edge of the village for their gardens. By now, strains of squash and gourd were being planted in the eastern woodlands; the varieties under cultivation were different from those domesticated in Middle America and may have derived from indigenous plants. Corn did not reach the woodlands from the Southwest until around AD 200, and the early strains were ill-suited to colder climes. Tobacco, however, was readily available, judging by the many pipes the Adena crafted of clay and stone.

A path dug in snow outlines the wings of a huge bird (above), created by ancient builders, that rises from a hillock in Iowa. At right is the most astonishing of ancient effigy mounds, a large earthen snake probably of Adena origin that writhes across a ridge in southern Ohio. It measures a quarter-mile from its coiled tail to its jaws, which contain an oval object, possibly an egg.

Adena weavers were proficient in the art of making clothing, blankets, bags, and mats from woven plant fibers. Lacking looms, they used their fingers to plait and twine the threads. In addition, potters fashioned cone-shaped or round-bottomed jars that they decorated by patting the soft surface with a corded wooden paddle before firing the vessel. Profiting by trade ties that brought them chunks of copper from glacial deposits in northern Michigan, sheets of mica from North Carolina, and marine shell from the Gulf, skilled artisans worked the raw materials with stone awls, drills, points, and scrapers to produce tightfitting bracelets, perforated gorgets that hung about the neck, and embossed effigies of falcons and other birds of prey.

In death as in life, the Adena treasured such belongings. The quantity and quality of the items that were buried with the honored dead proclaimed their standing in a society that was becoming increasingly stratified. Indeed, the mounds themselves gave evidence of assertive leadership and organization. From low memorial hillocks piled over the bones

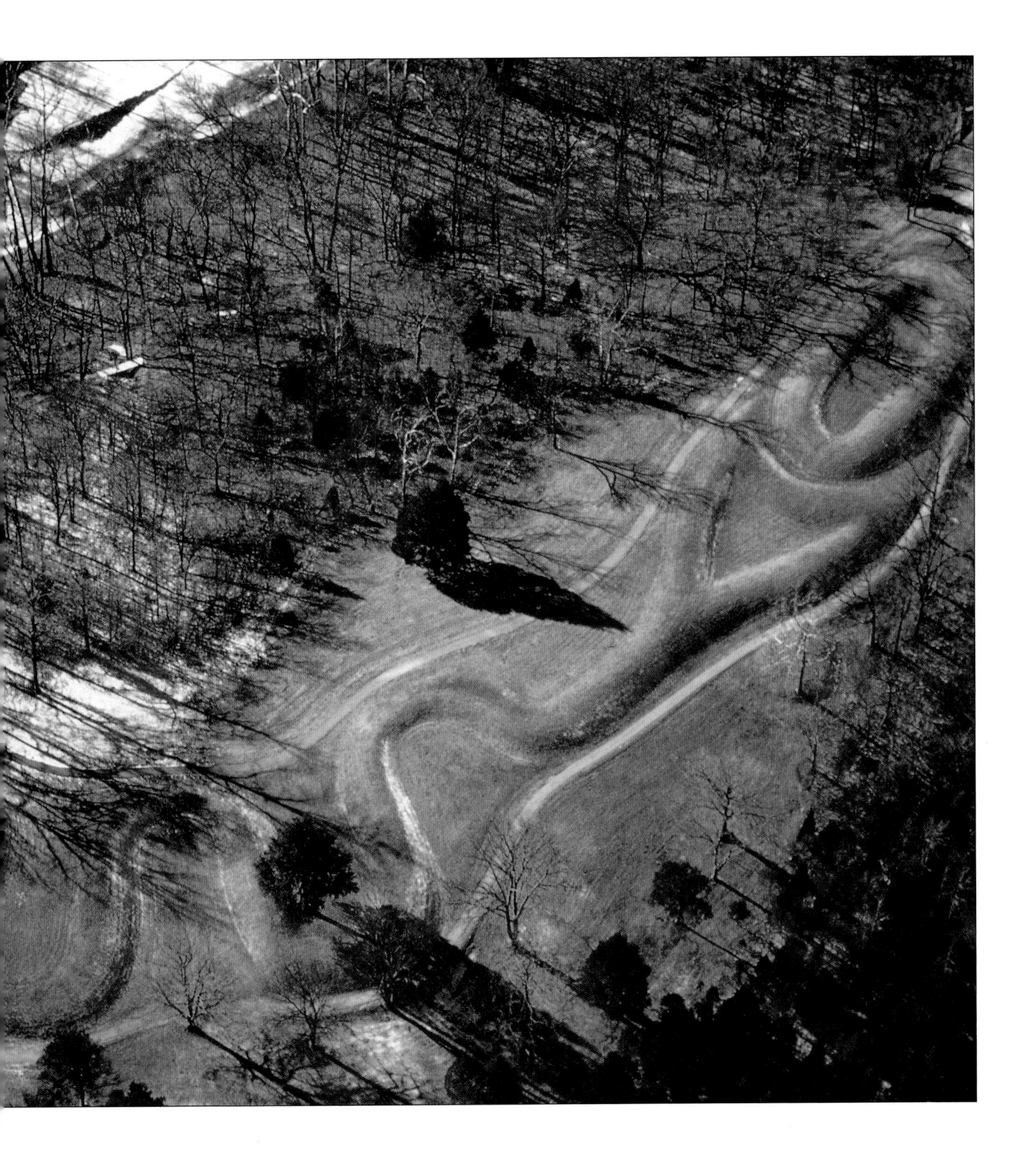

TALON OF A HAWK OR OTHER BIRD OF PREY

CROUCHING BEAR

of a single, cremated body, certain burial places grew ever larger and more complex until the greatest of them developed into monumental edifices. In other locations, the Adena raised up high, narrow ridges of earth in order to provide an enclosed space for ritual observances.

Only a people of great discipline and devotion could have sustained the labor such earthworks required. The seventy-foot-high Grave Creek Mound in West Virginia, for example, required 72,000 tons of earth. Theoretically, it would have taken thousands of Adena faithful more than five years of unstinting labor to pile it all up, basketful by backbreaking basketful. In practice, however, mammoth earthworks of this sort were typically built up in stages by small crews over long periods. Relays of Indians must have traveled periodically from their scattered villages to the construction sites, where they were provided with food and shelter—a communal effort that might continue for a century or more before the mound reached its final dimensions.

As each stage of a mound was completed, human remains would be committed to it. Thus the biggest mounds grew to contain several generations, with the earliest at the bottom. The deceased were either cremated or interred in the flesh. Ordinary folk usually were curled into round clay basins. Higher-ranking Adena were laid to rest on their backs in log tombs. Further honors were conferred on the elite by coating their bodies with red ocher or graphite and bedecking them with triumphs of Adena handiwork, including hundreds

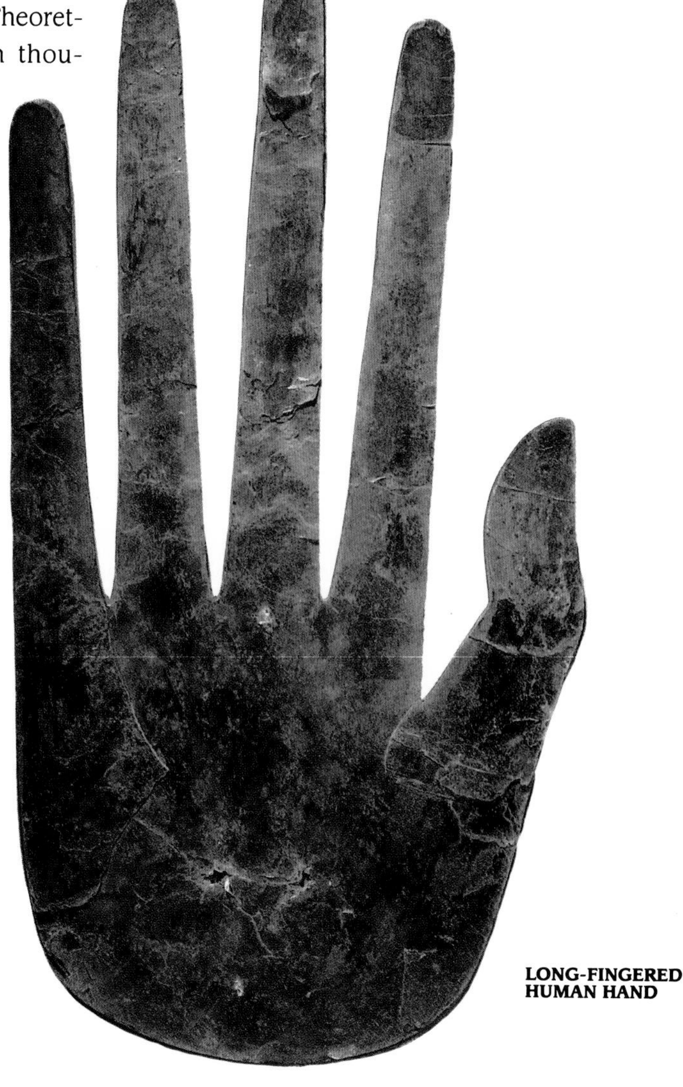
LONG-FINGERED HUMAN HAND

UNDULATING FIGURE OF A SNAKE

Creating triumphs of early art, Hopewell craftsmen employed sharp flint tools to cut thick, multilayered sheets of silvery mica into a wide variety of animal and human shapes, such as the vivid, translucent images shown on these pages. They were evidently worn as jewel-like pendants by members of the Hopewell elite.

of delicate shell beads, sheets of mica fashioned into attractive designs, and masks embedded with animal teeth and bones.

Not all the impressive earthworks constructed by the Indians of the northern woodlands were devoted exclusively to the dead. At a few early sites in present-day Ohio, and later in Wisconsin and environs, people created effigies in bas-relief of bear, foxes, tortoises, elk, buffalo, and birds. One such mound portrayed an eagle with a wingspread of 240 feet; another depicted a curious 150-foot-long man with two heads and his arms stretched wide. The strangest and most impressive of them all appeared in what is now Adams County, Ohio, where laborers heaped up earth to form a great serpent 5 feet high, 20 feet wide, and 1,254 feet long, uncoiling along a ridge. In the reptile's gaping jaws the designers placed an oval object resembling an egg—a symbol of generation or rebirth, perhaps, drawn from Indian mythology. Because these cryptic effigy mounds could be viewed properly only from on high, they were perhaps meant to be seen by gods or spirits thought to inhabit the sky.

The creators of the effigy mounds left few clues of their identity in the form of human remains or artifacts. Based on surrounding evidence, the Serpent Mound may have been crafted by the Adena, but most of the other monuments were apparently produced by peoples who came later and built on Adena accomplishments.

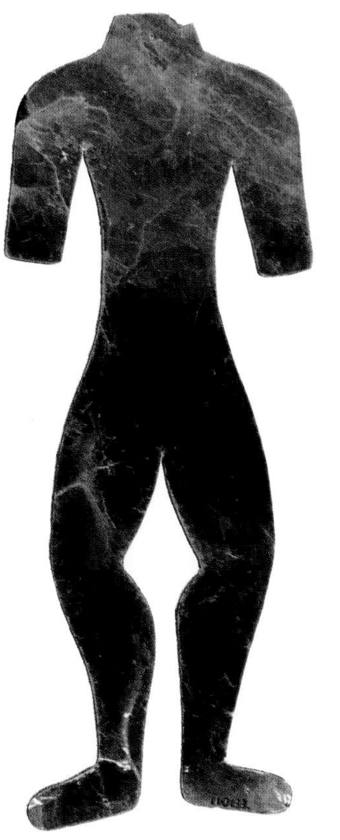

HEADLESS HUMAN FIGURE WITH TRUNCATED ARMS

Around 100 BC a distinct culture—known as Hopewell for a vast complex of mounds near the town of that name in south-central Ohio—began to emerge in the northern woodlands. Some Hopewell sites in Illinois were occupied by people who appeared to have a different cranial structure than the Adena, but such distinctions among the early Indians usually had more to do with the way they bound the heads of their infants than with anything genetic. Otherwise, the Hopewell had much in common with the Adena and may have been either neighbors or direct descendants who expanded on the older culture while preserving its essence.

By the first century AD, southern Ohio was a flourishing center of Hopewell activity, while another nexus was developing in southern Illinois; eventually, the culture's influence would be felt all the way from New England to the lower Mississippi. The Hopewell pursued many of the same customs as the Adena, but with greater vigor and elaboration. Hopewell earthworks were even larger and more complex, their burial ceremonies more intricate, their society more stratified, their arts and crafts more developed. They also were more enthusiastic traders than the Adena, building up a network that covered the whole of eastern North America and extended westward to the Rocky Mountains.

The Ohio Hopewell were particularly well situated for long-distance trade. In their dugout canoes, they could paddle and portage their way to Lakes Erie and Ontario and thence to the Saint Lawrence, Mohawk, and Hudson river valleys; or they could venture down the Ohio to the Mississippi, an avenue of exchange for goods traveling to and from the Gulf of Mexico, the western Great Lakes, and the plains and bluffs flanking the upper Missouri River. Included among the items they traded to others were slate, chert, freshwater pearls, and a variety of finished tools and ornaments; in exchange, they received prized materials for the use of their artisans, including copper mined near Lake Superior, turtle shells from the Gulf, chalcedony from North Dakota, and obsidian from a quarry in Wyoming that had been providing material for spearpoints ever since the days of the mammoth hunters.

Hopewell villages were bigger than the hamlets of the Adena, but at their largest, they still housed no more than a few hundred people each. Their circular or oval-shaped houses were probably built of flexible saplings that were set in the ground and then bent over to form a rounded roof covered with animal skins, tough sheets of elm bark, or mats of woven fiber. The typical settlement was an unassuming place, aswarm with dusty dogs and tumbling children in dry periods and transformed into a muddy quagmire when it rained. Most villages were positioned in lush river bottom lands where much of what the people needed lay close by. Nonetheless, the Hopewell appear to have emptied entire villages for a time in the late autumn and again in the early spring, when the populace foraged for plant life or game either to build up stocks for the winter or to replenish them afterward.

Like the Adena, the Hopewell had little need to devote great energy to working the land when they could draw so much nourishment from the surrounding forests. Here and there, they grew small amounts of corn

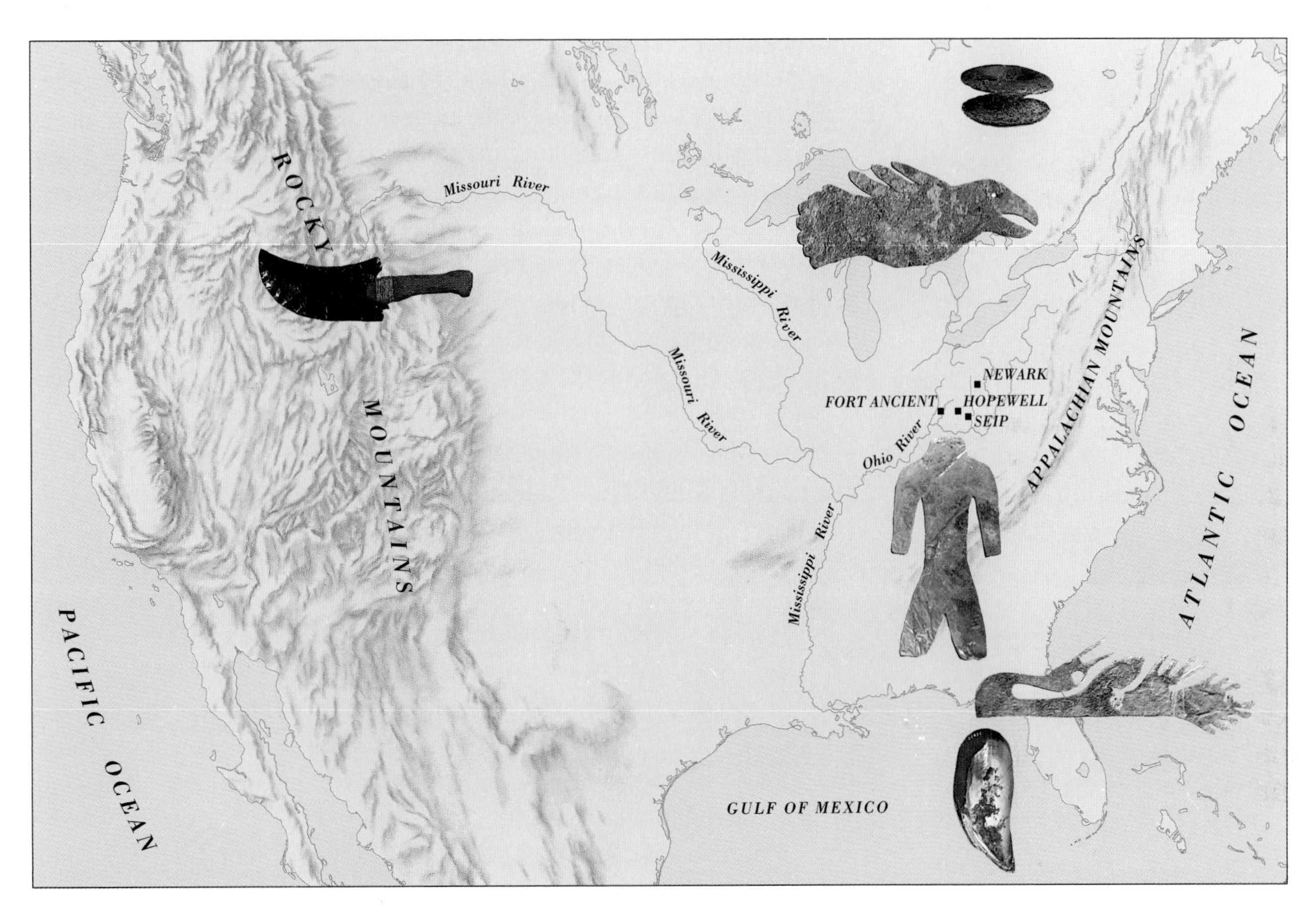

The extensive reach of the Hopewell Indians' trading network is shown in the map above, which also pictures some of the tools and other items made from the raw materials that the Hopewell obtained. The Hopewell paddled their canoes along North America's linked river systems, trading for conch and tortoise shells. From the mountains to the west came the hard obsidian that was used to make cutting blades and spearpoints. The Great Lakes area yielded copper, and Canada was the source of silver nuggets. The southern Appalachians supplied the mica that the Hopewell shaped into some of their loveliest ornaments.

in their gardens, but the kernels or seeds they cultivated were less important to their diet than nuts, fish, and meat. Hunters seeking skittish, solitary prey in the woods avoided the group hunting techniques favored by Plains Indians. Most often, an Indian hunted alone, creeping up on his quarry until he was close enough to hurl a spear. Sometimes, the hunter donned a deer head with antlers and mimicked the animal's browsing movements as he approached his target. The Hopewell, moreover, were canny trappers. Animals as large as deer could be taken in bent sapling snares, and smaller creatures could be captured in loop snares concealed along game trails and runs.

Judging by the customs of later woodland Indians, the men of the villages were probably responsible not only for hunting, fishing, and trading expeditions but also for felling trees and clearing land, as well as for crafting weapons, tools, canoes, snowshoes, and bark barrels for the storage of food. Alternatively, they might dig storage pits and line them with leather or bark to keep out moisture. The women, for their part, may have performed such essential tasks as smoking or drying meat and vegetables on racks set up outside the houses; tilling the gardens and maintaining the houses; collecting firewood and cooking meals over open fires; making pottery and weaving cloth; and gathering roots, berries, fruits, and nuts. In warm weather, women went bare breasted, with calf-length skirts belted at the waist, while men wore loincloths. In winter, both sexes wrapped themselves in furs and robes of tanned skins, or clothing woven from pliable vegetable fibers and painted in abstract designs. According to lifelike figurines crafted by Hopewell artists, women typically wore their hair in a long braid, while men tended to shave their heads except for a scalp lock or ceremonial topknot.

The routine of daily life was relieved by religious ceremonies in which the whole village participated, and by games and athletic contests. Men and boys likely ran footraces on the hard-packed earthen clearing before their domed huts and engaged in jumping or spear-throwing contests. Gambling with dice or marked sticks was a time-honored diversion. Children amused themselves with dolls of humans or animals made out of wood or bone, toy canoes and sleds, and tubes of bird bone that evidently served as straws both for playful youngsters and ailing adults. Storytelling must have occupied an important place in Hopewell life. As the narrator wove a spell, the rapt audience might puff on clay pipes, or sip an infusion of some kind. Besides tobacco, the villagers probably smoked other wild plants or barks, or brewed them to make a tea.

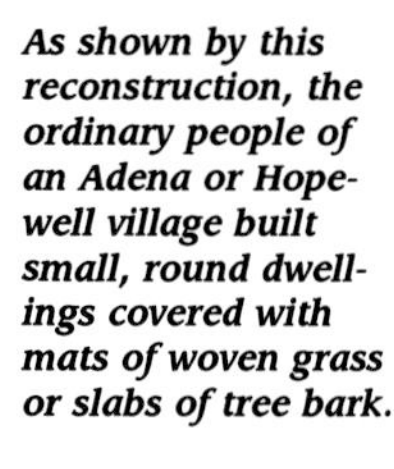

As shown by this reconstruction, the ordinary people of an Adena or Hopewell village built small, round dwellings covered with mats of woven grass or slabs of tree bark.

The great burial mounds that the Hopewell built drew laborers from a considerable distance and served as the focus of observances that symbolically united scattered settlements. In some locations, large numbers of mounds were enclosed within embankments that defined the sacred precincts. At the site in Ohio for which the Hopewell were named, for example, thirty-eight mounds were built within an enclosure covering 110 acres, forming a complex that must have been the ceremonial hub for the occupants of dozens of surrounding villages. Remarkably, the mounds within the complex were not constructed in stages. Each went up in a single protracted effort.

Such projects required deft coordination and commanding leadership. Hopewell chiefs whose influence extended over a considerable area evidently supervised the task and occupied a place of honor in the mounds. Burial customs varied from place to place. Among the Illinois Hopewell, individuals of the top rank were laid out at the center of a log crypt, while the bones of people of secondary importance who had died earlier were arrayed around them. Curiously, most of those accorded a central position in the crypt were mature males of above-average height. Perhaps they achieved prominence by dint of their size and prowess. They may have been avid hunters or warriors, for many developed an arthritic condition of the elbow, perhaps as a result of constantly hurling spears with the aid of atlatls. By contrast, the men buried around the leaders tended to have arthritis of the wrist, associated with repetitive hand movements of the sort engaged in by artisans.

Larger Hopewell structures such as the lodge shown below probably housed either artisans at work or village meetings. A double row of vertical posts framed the walls; inside, more posts supported beams that in turn held up a system of rafters—strips of wood bent so the roof curved. As with the simpler dwelling at left, the lodge had a hole in the grass or bark roof to vent smoke from a firepit dug in the packed-clay floor.

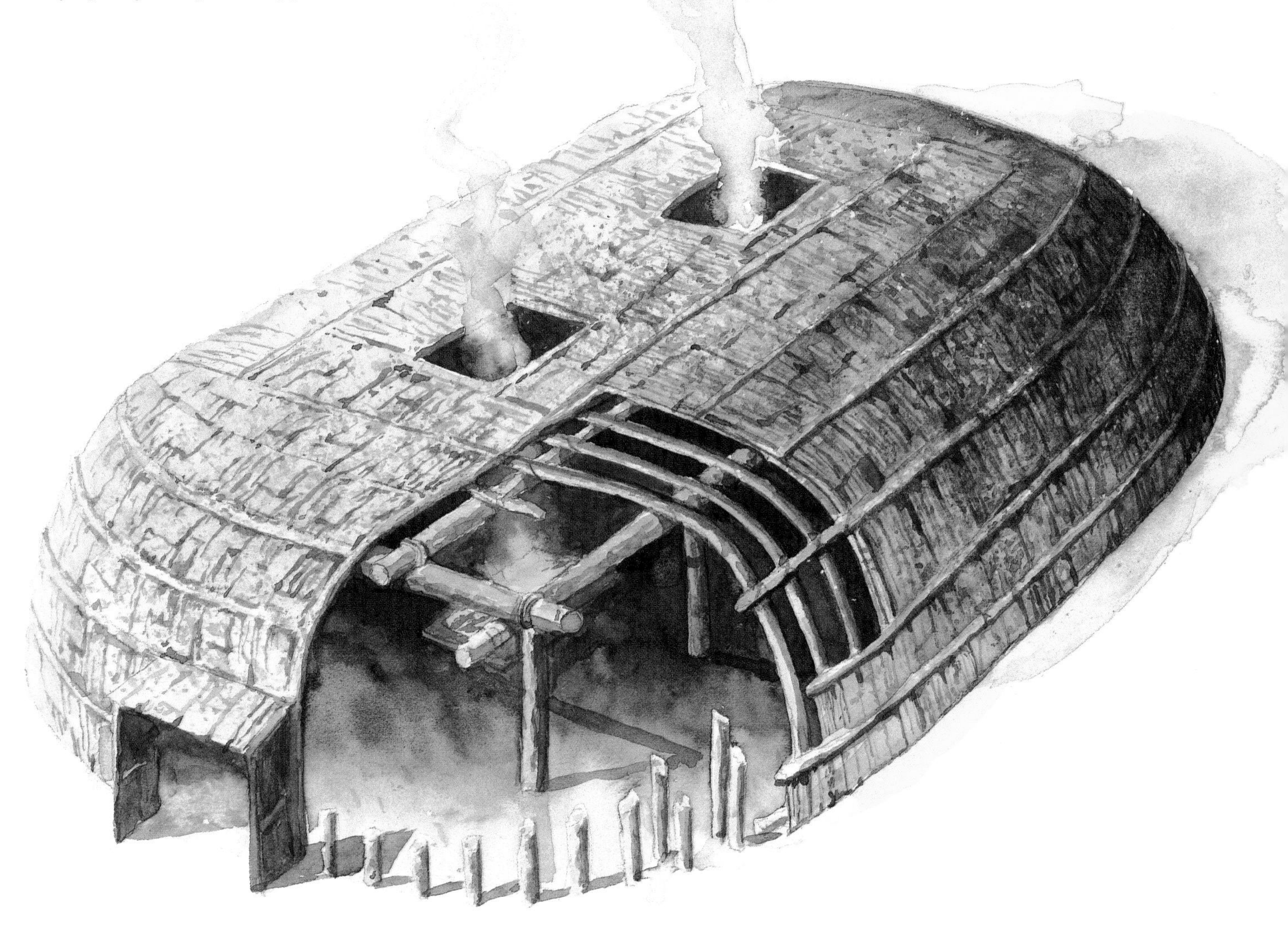

The Ohio Hopewell, who cremated most of their dead, distinguished the elite by burying them in the flesh and honoring them with a profusion of grave offerings. Typically, workers would prepare the burial site by clearing it of trees and brush, removing loose topsoil, and laying down a foundation of clay topped by sand or gravel. On that base they would erect a log mortuary house, sometimes containing several chambers. In a central chamber, the dead leader was extended full length in a rectangular log tomb. He might be alone or surrounded by the corpses of women and children who were evidently related to him. There were no signs of sacrifice; possibly those who accompanied the leader on his journey died at the same time as a result of infectious disease, or perhaps they perished earlier and were placed beside him at his death. Outside the central chamber, clay-lined crematory pits held the ashes of retainers or others who had died in the service of their leader. Once the chief was laid in his tomb and the grave goods were deposited, the complete mortuary structure was burned to the ground, after which long lines of workers carried earth in wicker baskets to dump on the glowing embers. The piling up of earth continued for weeks or even months, until the mound reached a height of up to forty feet.

Some Hopewell chiefs went to the grave along with veritable treasure troves. At the Seip Mound in Ross County, Ohio, mourners entombed four cherished adults in

Evoking the creatures of the forests around them, Hopewell carvers delicately sculpted the ceremonial stone pipes shown below in the likenesses of animals and birds. The arched rectangular bases, drilled through, formed the pipestems; a bowl cut in the creature's back or head held the tobacco.

AN ALERT, WATCHFUL HAWK

A BEAVER WITH EYES OF FRESHWATER PEARLS AND TEETH OF BONE INLAY

a log chamber, with two children lying transversely at their heads. All of them were enveloped from head to toe in gallons of freshwater pearls, among which were strewn tools and ornaments made of copper, mica, tortoiseshell, and silver. At another site located in Hamilton County, the deceased were endowed with 35,000 pearl beads, 12,000 individual pearls, 20,000 shell beads, nuggets of silver, and sheets of hammered copper. In still another vault at the great Hopewell complex, a tall young man was laid to rest beside a young woman bedecked not only with pearls but also with thousands of copper-covered wood and stone buttons. Both young people were adorned in copper bracelets, spool earrings, and breastplates, and fitted with artificial copper noses. To one side, the burial party placed a massive copper ax weighing twenty-eight pounds.

A GREAT BLUE HERON EATING A SMALL FISH

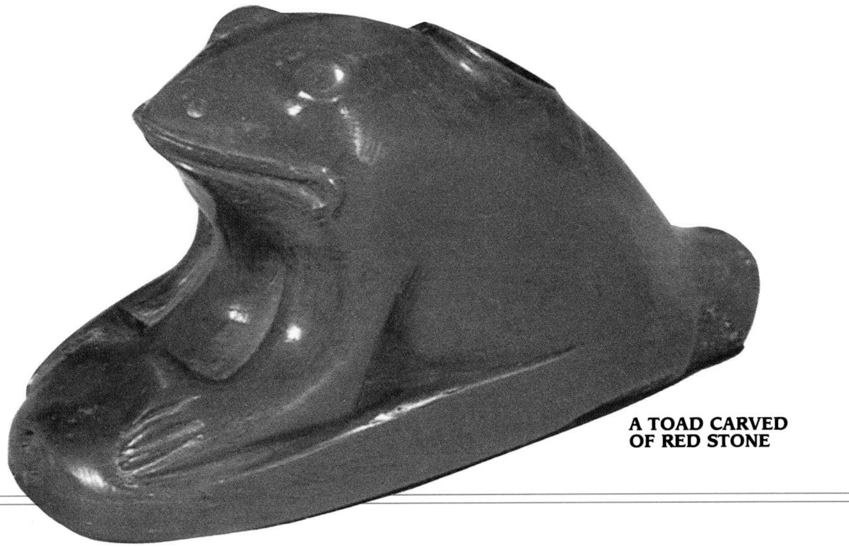

A TOAD CARVED OF RED STONE

The grave offerings showered on the chiefs and their retinues were the painstaking efforts of expert artisans, who must have devoted much if not all of their time to their specialties. Conceivably, they were recruited and trained by institutions akin to guilds that enjoyed elite patronage. However the Hopewell mastered their skills, they had few rivals among the early American Indians as potters, stone knappers, metalworkers, and sculptors. Their preferred metal was copper, which they fashioned into beads, gorgets, pendants, panpipes, swastikas, serpent heads, effigies of fish and birds, and myriad sheets that were embossed with

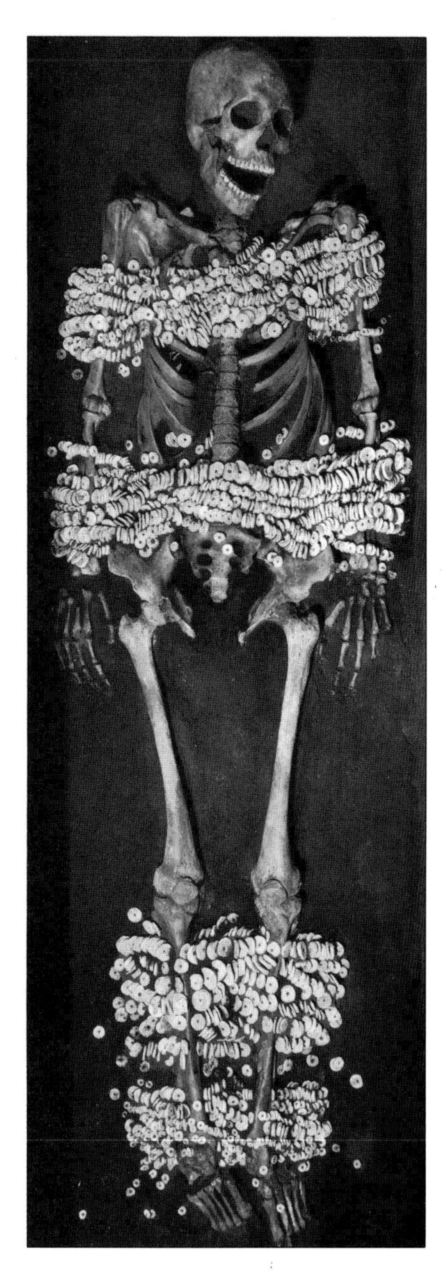

The skeleton of a young Mississippian woman who was buried in a grave mound in Wisconsin about the year 1200 is adorned at shoulders, waist, and legs by long strings of shell beads. The bones are assuredly those of an elite person; like the Adena and Hopewell peoples before them, the Mississippians interred precious goods with deceased members of the ruling class.

animal motifs and abstract designs. Unfamiliar with the process of smelting ore, they instead pounded and annealed the copper nuggets, sometimes hammering them into thin, malleable sheets, sometimes molding them into chunky tools such as hatchets, adzes, and awls. They hammered silver in the same fashion, creating glistening foil with which they covered buttons, earrings, or priestly wands.

Jewelers worked with a variety of materials, including tortoiseshell, bone, pearl, terra cotta, meteoric iron, quartz, and animal teeth, while stoneworkers rang variations on the age-old themes of their craft by chipping out prismatic ceremonial knives from chalcedony or obsidian, cutting thin sheets of mica to form lustrous silhouettes of humans or animals, and sculpting effigy pipes of soapstone or slate. Potters were equally imaginative, incising broad, shallow grooves in the damp clay with a stylus to create hypnotic geometric figures or evocative bird designs before firing the vessel at the same hearth that broiled meat and kept out the winter cold.

The convention of lavishing luxuries on the deceased was partly responsible for the maintenance of the extensive Hopewell trading system over the centuries. The same strong, steady demand for the handiwork of the artisans would not have prevailed had the wealth been hoarded and then passed on to successive generations. In addition, the system may have benefited the culture as a whole in other ways. Leaders who were due tribute probably watched over the stores of food and other goods and distributed them in times of deprivation. And on a spiritual level, the Hopewell people evidently regarded the prosperity of their chiefs in this life and the next as a good omen for the community.

About AD 400, for reasons that remain unclear, the fortunes of the Hopewell started to decline. The climate turned colder around that time, which may have rendered foraging and gardening less productive and reduced the surplus of goods that supported craftsmanship and trade. Possibly such environmental stress also increased hostilities between neigh-

A nineteenth-century painting of an early excavation shows a cross section of a burial mound with surprising accuracy. The sitting skeleton at top rests in a grave dug in the mound after it was completed. The nearby recumbent skeletons are those of an earlier burial. Bands of colored earth indicate successive layers that were added to the mound.

boring parties. Although the Indians of the region were not known to wage war on a large scale, armed bands sometimes turned against their neighbors. A few of the enclosures that were built by the Hopewell may have served as fortifications in unsettled times, and their burial sites contained evidence of violence—mangled corpses, and here and there amid the grave offerings a severed head or arm, claimed by a warrior chief

The whimsical jar created in the shape of a chubby leg, shown below, was fashioned of clay by an artist of the Mississippian culture.

from one of his captives as a trophy, perhaps, and taken with him to the grave. Whatever the natural or human ills that were responsible for sapping their strength, the Hopewell soon ceased their long-distance trading and massive mound building, leaving the eastern woodlands region without a dominant culture for several centuries.

The people who ultimately filled that gap were the so-called Mississippians, the builders of Cahokia, whose culture took root in the lower Mississippi Valley around the year 700 and eventually exerted influence across much of the eastern half of the North American continent. In the production of crafts and the development of trade, they were worthy successors to the Hopewell. What set them apart, however, was their mastery of agriculture; they were the first intensive farmers in the woodlands, cultivating corn and other crops on a grand scale. This breakthrough in securing nourishment from the soil enabled them to live in larger settlements and devote more of their energy to the building of great ceremonial centers.

Mississippian society bore some resemblance to contemporary Middle American civilizations and the Hohokam culture of the Southwest in that the fruits of intensive agriculture and other pursuits were funneled to an elite, who presided over lavish rituals associated with massive pyramid mounds and plazas. Nevertheless, the Mississippian chiefs almost certainly derived such customs from indigenous woodland traditions such as the Hopewell. Over time, some artistic and religious motifs from Mexico and environs reached the woodlands along coastal and inland trade routes, but the principal debt of the Mississippians to the Southwest was horticultural—in particular, new strains of corn that reached their settlements from that direction around the eighth century. Up to that time, the cultivation of maize had been limited to those areas to the east that enjoyed a growing season of 200 days or more. The new strains required only 120 frost-free days. Consequently, corn could be planted farther north than before, and in the southern regions, two bountiful harvests were possible each year. Eventually, the Mississippians adopted another southwestern staple—beans, which in conjunction with corn supplied all the protein that the human diet required. The woodland Indians now had in place what some of their descendants would call the Three Sisters: corn, beans, and squash. No longer were they so dependent on hunting and gathering.

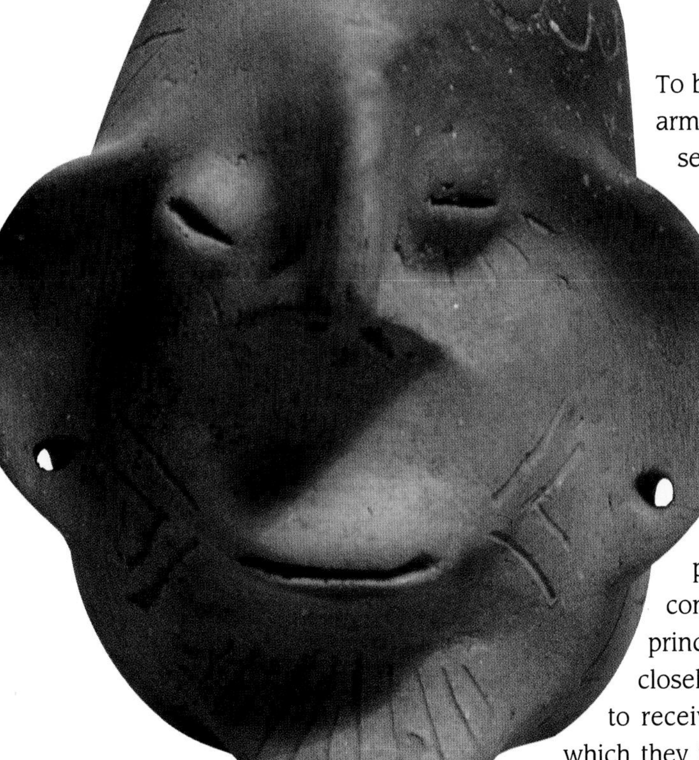

To be sure, the Mississippians remained ardent hunters, armed as they were with a recent innovation that represented a significant advance over the spear—the bow and arrow. Hunters were now capable of striking at their quarry from a greater distance, and with greater accuracy and frequency. The earliest Spanish explorers would be astounded at the abilities of the woodland archers; the Indians could launch three or four arrows with deadly effect before the Europeans could manage to load and fire a single shot from their ponderous crossbows and harquebuses.

So important was agriculture to the Mississippian people that they evolved a cult extolling the sun—considered the guarantor of bountiful harvests—as their principal deity. Evidently, their chiefs were priest-rulers, closely associated with the power of the sun and entitled to receive a portion of the harvest in the form of tribute, which they then stored for the use of their own households as well as for redistribution to the populace. In addition to seasonal agrarian ceremonies, the Mississippians practiced hunting rituals that were similar to those of the Adena and Hopewell.

Another jar, discovered in Louisiana and dating back to Mississippian times, is made in the form of a comical slant-eyed human face.

Although intensive farming helped generate large towns such as Cahokia that boasted many thousands of inhabitants and covered hundreds of acres, most of the Mississippians lived in small, dispersed villages populated by fewer than 100 people. Houses were constructed in a simple fashion; they had pole frames with wattled walls of flexible cane or reed and gabled roofs of thatch. In some farmsteads, the villagers had both cold- and warm-weather dwellings. The cold-weather houses had an internal hearth and storage pits and might be plastered with mud to keep the wind out; the warm-weather structures were generally larger and breezier, and the occupants kept them cool by cooking outdoors.

On the outskirts of the villages, the fields of corn stretched away, dotted with blackened spars where the trees had first been girdled to die in the spring, then torched in the fall, leaving ashes to enrich the soil. When earth that had been prepared in this way was exhausted, the villagers simply moved a short distance to a new location. As was later the custom among Indian tribes that followed in the footsteps of the Mississippians, women were probably expected to watch over the crops, wielding dig-

ging sticks or flint hoes. Around the long rows of corn, they planted beans and squash. The Bean Sister, they knew, would twine about the stalks of the Corn Maiden, using her for support, while the Squash Sister would spread her tendrils along the ground, choking out weeds and providing shade to keep the earth moist.

In small towns and large, life revolved around the flat-topped mounds that served as bases for temples and other ceremonial structures. The typical settlement might have one such truncated pyramid, while towns on the order of Cahokia might boast dozens of them. Following ancient precedent, some of the mounds served as burial grounds. The Cherokee Indians—one of the tribes to emerge subsequently in the area that was dominated by the Mississippians—preserved a legend of how a small burial mound was raised by their ancestors. The Cherokees told of men in the distant past who laid out a circle of stones on the ground around a flame. Next to the flame the mound builders placed the body of a great chief, adorned with beads of seven colors and the right wing of an eagle. A priest invoked all the diseases known to the tribe so that if the tomb fell into the hands of an enemy, he would not live to return home. Then people brought earth in baskets and built up the tomb, taking care to leave a hole in the center so that the flame within could be fed eternally.

In fact, the Mississippians did not actually build mounds in this fashion. The sacred flames that they lit burned in a temple situated on top of

Looming eerily in the mist, a half-dozen of the twenty temple mounds remaining at Moundville rise above the surrounding Alabama plain. The Indians of Moundville, the second-largest Mississippian settlement after Cahokia, made some of the finest of that culture's art, such as the bowl below, carved from hard, greenish diorite in the shape of a bird—perhaps a crested wood duck.

the mound, for example, not inside the structure. Nonetheless, the legend of the Cherokees faithfully described the purpose of the ancient mound-building ritual—to glorify the chief—and illuminated other important details, noting that the mound and its enclosures had to be built on the "level bottom lands by the river in order that the people might have the smooth ground for their dances and ball plays and might be able to go down to water during the dance." Indeed, the Mississippians made use of the sacred enclosure for other purposes besides mourning; they also celebrated festivals there and exchanged goods in the plaza.

As was frequently the case among the Adena and Hopewell, the Mississippians constructed their mounds in stages. In order to make room for the remains of recent leaders, the Indians would periodically level the wood-and-mud temples on the summit, add another layer of earth, and raise a fresh temple complex. The immense, 102-foot-tall central mound in Cahokia—which was wider at its base than the Great Pyramid of Egypt—was built in a dozen or more phases over the course of two centuries. Each stage demanded the labor of thousands of Indians hauling sixty-pound baskets of earth.

The temples located atop the Cahokia edifice and lesser pyramids were forbidden to all but priests and the guardians of the sacred flame—who, according to tradition, faced death if they failed to nourish the fire.

Inside, the temples were decorated with strands of pearls, pendants of copper and shell, and headdresses of dyed turkey feathers that were suspended from the rafters. On an altar rested painted wooden and stone statuettes of departed ancestors, seated on folded legs with hands on their knees, their mouths half-open, and their eyes agape as if perceiving things beyond the range of living eyes. On burial days, the deceased would be placed in a cedar litter on the clay floor, his face painted, his body enveloped in feathers and furs, his hair agleam with copper, mica, and pearls. At Cahokia, if the ceremony marked the passing of a great priest-ruler, scores of people might be rendered unconscious by ingesting a potent plug of tobacco and then sacrificed to accompany the deceased on his voyage to the hereafter.

People who had been close to the priest-ruler may have considered it a duty and an honor to give up their lives and join him in the next world, but others may have been captives or other hapless victims who were rounded up for the occasion. The passing of one apparent priest-ruler at Cahokia occasioned the sacrifice of more than fifty women, whose corpses were neatly arranged in pits that had been dug into the floor of a burial mound. Near them lay four men—enemy prisoners, perhaps—whose heads and hands had been cut off. The deceased ruler himself was put to rest on a bed of 20,000 shell beads and surrounded by the richly adorned bodies of six men and women, possibly close relatives, who may also have been put to death. In some tombs, the Mississippians placed effigy jars depicting the heads of enemies with their eyes closed and their mouths sewn shut. Left behind at a few places were ceremonial knives that may have served as instruments to behead captives.

In order to secure lavish tribute in life as in death, a Mississippian chief might do battle with his neighbors, aided by warriors who sought to improve their social standing by demonstrating their bravery. The victorious party would then exact a periodic levy of crops, goods, or laborers from the losing side. Through such methods, the leaders of some large ceremonial centers eventually extended their domains to include villages dozens of miles away. Beyond a certain distance, however, the tribute system ceased to be practical, and nothing approaching an empire developed in the eastern woodlands.

Marble figures of a glowering man (right) and woman probably represented ancestor gods who guarded the shrine on top of a temple mound of the settlement in Etowah, near Cartersville, Georgia, where they were found. Both statues are two feet tall and have been painted. Several similar pairs of figures have been discovered in mounds in Mississippian sites located in the Southeast.

Among the regional centers to reach heights of influence rivaling that of Cahokia was the site known as Moundville, situated in present-day Alabama along the Black Warrior River. Established sometime after the year 1000, the main plaza grew to contain twenty mounds covering an area of nearly 300 acres. Perhaps 3,000 Indians resided around this walled complex, which had three large pits excavated by laborers as they fetched earth for the mounds; at a later date, the pits were evidently filled with water and stocked with fish to help feed the populace. In outlying areas lay smaller, subordinate centers—single mounds surrounded by villages whose inhabitants had been drawn into Moundville's ceremonial web either by force or by other inducements. The vast scale of the Moundville plaza and the extravagance of the grave offerings heaped on its chiefs suggest that people of the neighboring villages paid homage to those leaders both in the form of labor and in the form of raw materials or crafted articles.

Although they gave up treasure, toil, and even blood to glorify the dead, the Mississippians were far from being a morbid people. Like the Indians who later inhabited the Southeast, they evidently believed that the world they were born into was just one level of a complex universe. Below lay a chaotic, watery underworld, associated with cold-blooded creatures such as snakes and lizards; but above stretched a radiant upper world, symbolized by eagles, falcons, and other soaring raptors and ruled by the nourishing spirit of the sun. By raising up mounds, tending sacred flames, and exalting their leaders, the Mississippians came a step closer to that pure fire in the sky.

As with all ambitious cultures, however, the luster of Mississippian society eventually began to fade. Major building at Cahokia ceased during the thirteenth century, and other important centers declined around the same time. Only a few pockets of the culture lingered on to astound the first European witnesses. In a sense, the Mississippians may have been too successful for their own good. The maize-and-bean horticulture that they practiced likely generated population densities as much as five times those allowed by the Hopewell subsistence pattern. As settlements grew larger and denser, however, health risks associated with poor sanitation increased. Conceivably, epidemics so reduced the population around some centers that their leaders could no longer maintain the costly ceremonial complexes. Furthermore, the stratified nature of Mississippian society might have led to destructive tensions between those who were born to a high station and ambitious commoners who sought to supplant them. Just how complex that society could be was revealed in remarkable detail in the seventeenth century when French explorers encountered one of the last remnants of the great mound-building culture—the Natchez chiefdom of the lower Mississippi Valley.

The Natchez people, by the time French observers came in close contact with them, had already been reduced by the advent of European-carried diseases to a population of about 3,500, inhabiting a string of villages along Saint Catherine Creek near the modern-day town in Mississippi that bears their name. In spite of the devastating losses, their ceremonial life continued to flourish, offering insights into the customs that prevailed during earlier times. The Natchez were a sun-worshiping theocracy, with a sedentary life founded on the cultivation of corn. The defining myth of Natchez life described the descent to earth of the son of the all-powerful solar deity, and how this son brought culture to the Natchez in the form of laws, rituals, and crafts. His mission accomplished, the god's divine son retired into a stone that was ever afterward held sacred in the principal Natchez temple.

Leadership of the Natchez was invested in a chieftain, known as the Great Sun, who wielded the power of life and death over his subjects. His relatives exercised all the administrative authority in the tribe. The Great Sun himself had his home on the main temple mound, while lesser Suns resided close at hand. Various idols and holy objects were enshrined at the great temple—figurines that had been carved from stone or fashioned in clay, the heads and tails of rattlesnakes, a number of stuffed owls, and the jawbones of several large fish. The Great Sun worshiped before the idols every morning and evening and then announced what they foretold to his assembled people.

Below the ruling class of Suns was a class of nobles, and below that a class of honored men, or lesser nobles. At the bottom of this stratified society were the hard-working commoners, known by a contemptuous Natchez term translated loosely as Stinkards. Once a month, on ceremo-

IN PRAISE OF THE DEAD

Among the objects that they fashioned to venerate their ancestors, the ruling families of Mississippian Indians included images of the dead and ritual sacrifice—so much so that they fostered what has been labeled a cult of death. But their artistic creations, such as those shown on these pages, portray not only slayings and similar grisly themes but also celebrations of life, especially the birds and animals the Mississippians clearly revered. Above all, the Indians seem to have worshiped the life-giving sun, of which the temple fire was considered a reflection. In fact, among the Natchez, descendants of the Mississippians, the chief was called the Great Sun and was honored as a representative of the solar deity who had handed down the laws and customs that all the people were to live by forever.

A small gorget fashioned of marine shell shows a richly garbed warrior-chief holding a war club in one hand and the severed head of an enemy in the other.

A ceramic beaker discovered at Moundville, Alabama, is incised with a stylized skull and some bones that evidently symbolized the remains of an honored ancestor.

A pair of hands carved of marine shell shows a cross-in-circle design that may have been the mark of a chief claiming descent from the sun or other heavenly deity.

The face of a dead person, lips curled back and eyes closed, is modeled on this earthenware pot from Arkansas, which probably depicted the head of an ancestor. Incised on the forehead may be a combined symbol of sun and wind.

A stone paint palette portrays what was likely the hand of the sun god, with a blazing eye in the palm surrounded by a ring of knotted, sacred snakes.

Grimacing fiercely, a warrior clubs his victim's face while holding him by the scruff of his neck. This restored ceramic pipe was found at a western outpost of Mississippian culture, the Spiro Mound in Oklahoma.

Elaborately engraved, a conch shell drinking cup shows a warrior costumed as a falcon with a beak, wing feathers, and tail—as well as such human ornaments as a necklace and heart-shaped apron.

Made of a large seashell, this mask, found at the Spiro site in Oklahoma, portrays a man's face with lines that suggest lightning. Such mask gorgets were evidently sources of power and may have been worshiped as embodiments of ancestor valor or supernatural might.

nial feast days, all of the Natchez people went to the temple to pay tribute to their exalted ruler. He generally appeared before them wearing a royal crown made of swan's feathers, seated in a litter that was carried by eight bearers. On the rare occasions when he walked, it was on mats spread before him by retainers so that his feet never touched the bare earth. Nor was he obliged to use his hands very often. If he wished to give the remains of his meal to relatives, reported a French Jesuit priest, "he pushed the dishes to them with his feet."

The Natchez reportedly built their temple mounds high so that the earthly Sun and the heavenly sun could converse more easily. "Every morning," wrote the Jesuit, the "great chief honors by his presence the rising of his elder brother, and salutes him with many howlings as soon as he appears above the horizon. Afterward, raising his hand above his head and turning from the east to the west, he shows him the direction that he must take in his course."

The ritual that surrounded the death of a Natchez luminary was reminiscent of the somber sacraments carried out in the heyday of the Mississippian culture. Following the death of the Great Sun's younger brother—a man named Tattooed Serpent—his two wives, his medicine man, his head servant, and his pipe bearer were all ritually strangled. So, too, were several old women who evidently believed that the time had come to offer up their lives.

The most noteworthy feature of Natchez society was the manner in which it reinvigorated itself through a systematic mingling of blood among the classes—a characteristic that may offer an explanation for the unusual longevity of the chiefdom. For all the apparent social stratification, every grade of nobility, including the Great Sun himself, was obliged to wed common Stinkards. And in this matrilineal system, only the children of female Suns married to Stinkards were permitted to maintain the highest rank; the children of male Suns were demoted one step to the rank of noble. As a consequence, the son of the Great Sun would not be able to inherit the mantle of his father, since he would be only a noble. The successor to the Great Sun usually was the son of one of his sisters, who had married a Stinkard.

And so it went, down through the ranks of the Natchez people. The children of female nobles remained nobles themselves, while those of male nobles became mere honored men. And the sons of male honored men, alas, became Stinkards. Most lowborn Stinkards remained Stinkards, of course, but they could dream of marrying high for the sake

In a final glimpse of the great temple mound culture, a chief of the Natchez Indians, wearing a crown of swan feathers, rides in a litter carried by eight servants in this early-eighteenth-century sketch made by a French explorer of Mississippi and Louisiana, Antoine du Pratz. The Natchez were originally a Mississippian people and maintained the culture's sun-worshiping religion and rigid caste system of chiefs, nobles, and obedient common people.

of their children—although they themselves stood to gain nothing from the alliance. The Stinkard who married a Sun woman was still a Stinkard. He was not permitted to eat with his Sun wife and was required to remain standing while in her presence; if he offended her, he might be executed and replaced by another of his class.

The effect of this remarkable system was to guarantee a steady transfusion of new blood at all levels of society. There was even a possibility that commoners could rise to a higher level on their own merits, if they showed exceptional prowess in warfare. Certainly, the Natchez proved to be a stubbornly valiant people, the last champions of the great mound-building tradition. They were outmatched by European weaponry, however. In 1731, in a desperate battle, the French virtually wiped them out and sold the survivors into slavery. The Natchez were destined to go, a Jesuit piously declared, because "it appears that God wishes that they yield their place to new peoples."

In one form or another, however, woodland culture had long ago branched out, and some of those branches would continue to bear fruit. As early as the tenth century, migrants from the eastern forests had begun to grow corn and beans in fertile areas of the Great Plains stretching from the present-day Dakotas to Texas. These Indian settlers, like later homesteaders of European origin, may well have faced violent opposition from nomadic Plains dwellers, for some of their hamlets were surrounded by protective dry moats and palisades. Yet they persevered, supplementing their farming with occasional bison hunting. Not until the appearance of the horse and firearms made the pursuit of buffalo more rewarding did largely sedentary tribes such as the Dakota Sioux abandon their villages and take up the nomadic ways of other Plains Indians.

Staring intently at the photographer, members of a Choctaw family sit on the porch of their home in Mississippi in a picture taken in 1908. The woman at right grinds corn with mortar and pestle, tools that may have been passed down by people of the ancient Mississippian culture. Along with the Creek, Chickasaw, and Cherokee tribes, the Choctaw are thought to be direct descendants of the Mississippian temple mound builders.

Other prominent outposts of woodland culture arose in the Northeast, where traditions that had been nurtured in the warmer river valleys to the south and west gradually took hold. By AD 1000 villagers there were cultivating the Three Sisters, hunting deer and other quarry with bows and arrows, and building permanent settlements within palisades. Over many generations, a successful blend of farming, foraging, trade, and territorial expansion through either warfare or diplomacy led to the emergence of assertive Indian nations such as the Iroquois. But whether they coalesced into large societies or recognized ties to only a few neighboring hamlets along isolated streams or estuaries, the Indians of the eastern woodlands were heirs to the same bountiful legacy, one granted to those who pursued the promise of the sunlit fields without forgetting the lessons of the forest.

Tapering mummylike forms cover part of a 140-foot-long canyon wall in Utah known as the Great Gallery. Possibly 2,000 years old, this mural is one of the largest surviving examples of rock art in North America.

A LEGACY ON STONE

Inspired by unknown impulses, Indians of North America have left various designs on the canyons, cliffs, and boulders of their native landscapes. Many of these pictures, incised or painted, have survived to the present day, especially those that

were created in the arid Southwest where the climate has helped to preserve them.

The mysterious rock art drawings include ghostly human forms, wary game animals, abstractions with spirals, and meandering lines. It could be that they were designed to propitiate supernatural forces and ensure a group's general prosperity. Works depicting masked figures, elaborate headdresses, and richly decorated clothing are probably related to ceremonies conducted by shamans. And various geometric signs have been linked to recordkeeping or to the marking of cyclical natural events, such as the summer solstice. Only the images remain—evidence of the Indians' desire to express themselves through art.

ANIMATED IMAGES

ALASKA

UTAH

The figures found in rock art range from simple faces with no outline (upper left) to complex depictions of warriors holding shields (right). One image that appears throughout the Southwest is the humpbacked flute player (far lower left), often associated with the supernatural. The form has been labeled Kokopelli after a Hopi kachina, which it resembles.

ARIZONA

NEW MEXICO, AD 1400-1500

TEXAS, 4000-3000 BC

NEW MEXICO, AD 1400-1500

MYSTERIES OF THE ABSTRACT

Rows of slashes on the side of a rock in Utah probably represent an ancient form of recordkeeping. Abstract shapes are by far the most common type of rock art.

The incised design at right, found in California, resembles many creations of the Maya of Mexico and Guatemala.

Depictions of human hands, some life-size and others larger, decorate the lichen-covered surface of a boulder in New Mexico. Although handprints such as these appear in almost every major rock art area in North America, their meaning remains a puzzle.

PORTRAYING THE ANIMAL WORLD

ARIZONA, AD 1200-1400

MINNESOTA

BAJA CALIFORNIA, MEXICO

WASHINGTON STATE

The Indians may have created animal figures, such as the bighorn sheep carved into the seven-foot-high basalt boulder (opposite), as a means of increasing the game supply, or to record a tally of animals killed during a hunt. It may be that some animal portraits represent spiritual guardians or, in the case of the pregnant whale (lower center), images meant to promote fertility.

CALIFORNIA

For a period of nine centuries or more, generations of Indians left their marks on the face of this twenty-foot-wide boulder in Utah. Pictured on the surface known as Newspaper Rock is a miscellany of handprints, animal tracks, bison, bighorn sheep, footprints, and abstract elements dating from approximately AD 900 to the eighteenth century. The severely weathered, man-shaped figure with a weapon (top center) is the oldest image on the rock. The horse and rider (center) were not executed until the mid-1600s, after Spanish explorers brought the horse to the Americas.

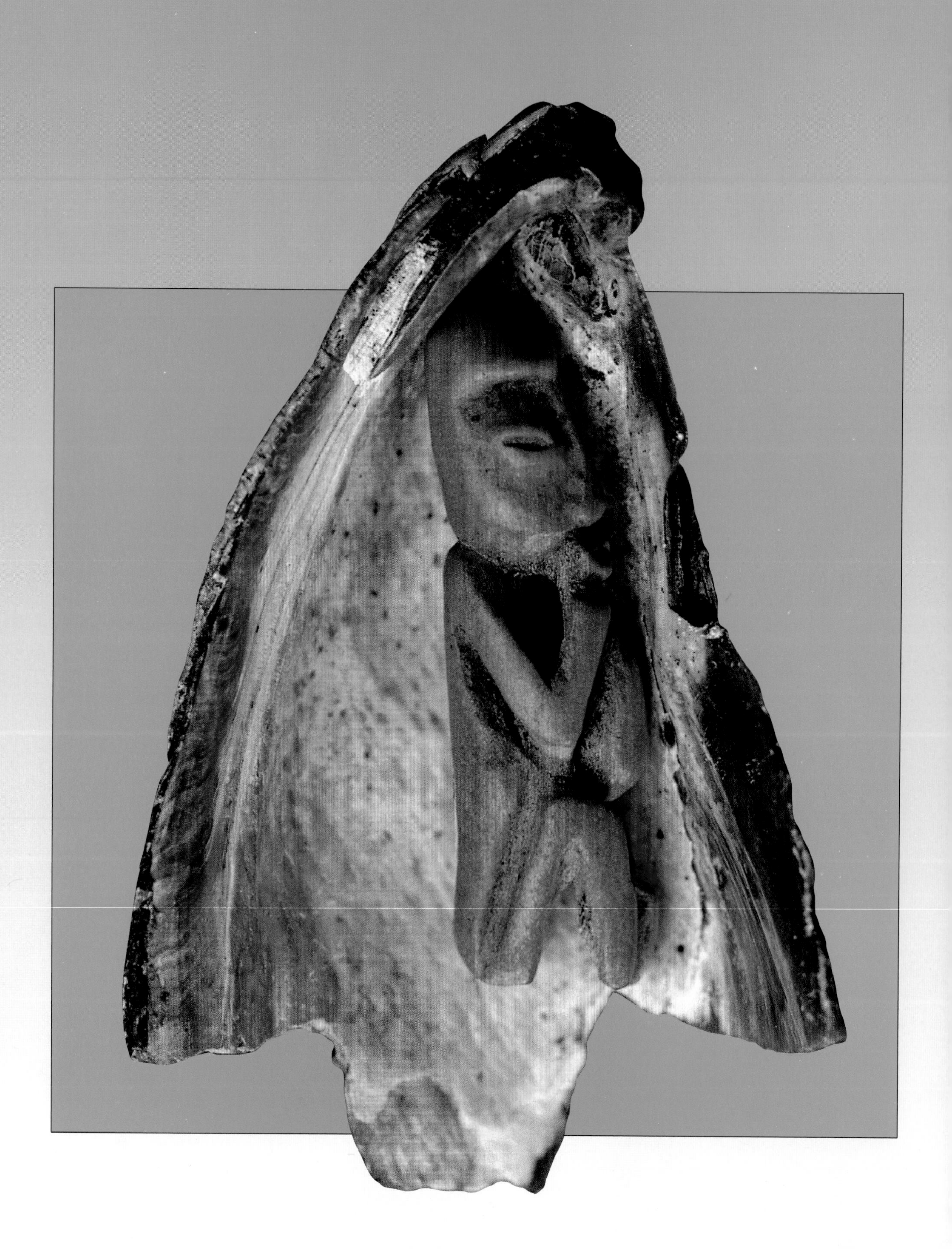

4

THE WHALE HUNTERS

A bone figurine nestled fetuslike in a mussel shell was created some five centuries ago by an Indian from Ozette, a village on the coast of present-day Washington State. The object evokes legends of the Pacific Northwest that human life dawned in a seashell. One such creation story attests that a drop of mucus from the nose of a weeping mother fell into a shell and evolved as an infant.

A June rain pelted the oceanside village of Ozette, hissing on the sandy beach and spattering against dugout canoes that had been hauled beyond the reach of the Pacific swell. Inside the cedar long houses that stood in two rows by the shore, the inhabitants had put aside their day's work. In one long house, three blanket-weaving looms stood idle; in another, rolls of freshly stripped cedar bark littered the floor, waiting for women to split, dry, and store the fibers for weaving into clothing or baskets. Approximately thirty people from several families lived in each of the houses, cooking their meals at hearths in the communal center area and sleeping in partitioned compartments on wooden ledges along the walls.

A prestigious whaler and his family occupied the corner of one building. Their living space was crowded with the tools of his trade: long, heavy harpoon shafts and baskets of harpoon tips. Wooden storage boxes contained his everyday possessions, but some of his riches were proudly displayed, including seashells obtained in trade with distant coastal tribes and an ornately carved model of a whale's dorsal fin, inlaid with hundreds of otter teeth.

Sometime during the night, the earth swallowed the whaler's wealth. A steep, muddy bluff behind the village, sodden with rain, suddenly gave way. The sliding hillside enveloped the house, and at least five others, under ten feet of wet clay. Most of the inhabitants escaped the disaster, but their belongings were lost, apparently forever.

The people of Ozette could not prevail against the mud slide, which occurred around AD 1580, but they did not let it drive them from their home on Washington State's Olympic Peninsula. Their ancestors had occupied the long, sheltered beach, and defended it against encroaching tribes, for perhaps 1,000 years—or, as their legend had it, "since the first Daylight"—because it was the closest canoe-launching site to the migration routes of two important food sources, the California gray whale and the northern fur seal. The people of Ozette knew themselves as Qwidicca-atx, "people who live on the cape by the rocks and the sea gulls." Their Indian neighbors—and white settlers who arrived centuries

later—knew them as Makah, "generous with food." It was a generosity made possible by the bounty of the ocean and forest of the Pacific Northwest, which the Makah had long exploited both wisely and well.

In time, the mud slide faded into legend. Nearly four centuries after it occurred, however, the same elements that had buried the houses conspired to expose them. Storm waves and driving rain ate away at the mud, until someone in the village noticed a strange canoe paddle, almost new, protruding from the hillside. At the first opportunity, the site was carefully explored, and it yielded a wealth of articles that had been preserved in pristine condition by the mud—harpoon points still smelling of the spruce pitch used to cement them to their shafts, mattresses of plaited cattail reeds, blankets woven of cedar strands and dog fur.

The mud slide at Ozette had created a virtual time capsule; the recovery of it offered a uniquely detailed portrait of life as it existed in an Indian village before the first contact with the Europeans. As the discovery confirmed, the Makah—like other tribes that settled along the Northwest Coast such as the Nootka, Tlingit, Kwakiutl, and Haida—had developed large, complex communities and intricate crafts without the impetus of agriculture. Instead, they had found permanence in their lives by patiently harvesting the sea, seeking its blessings with the same faith and diligence that Indians in other parts of North America had devoted to the land.

Just beyond the distinctively shaped Cannonball Island lie the secluded mainland ruins of Ozette, buried in a mud slide 400 years ago. More than 55,000 artifacts were unearthed from the site on Washington's Olympic Peninsula. They included a wooden club (above) used for killing seals, which in profile is seal-shaped, but when viewed frontally is a man's head.

From the Bering Strait to Baja California, the Pacific Coast offered abundant rewards to the first Americans. But the richest gleanings were to be found in the fog-shrouded coves and estuaries that extended from Oregon to southern Alaska. There, nature proved especially generous, nourishing the growth of sizable settlements.

When nomads from Siberia first ventured across the land bridge to the New World, just about all of the Northwest above central Washington State was covered by ice that reached to the edge of the ocean. As the glacial mass dwindled, however, it left behind a bountiful environment for fish, game, and foragers. Dominating this long, verdant coast was a prominent spine of volcanic mountains. In the north, along the Gulf of Alaska, the mountains descended nearly to the sea, leaving a narrow habitable shoreline that was cut by icefalls.

Just as their ancestors did before them, twentieth-century Makah women clean halibut and prepare it for drying on the shore of Neah Bay. The women leave the entrails on the beach for the tide to reclaim and throw the bones into the sea, to ensure that the fish will be born again the next year.

Farther south lay a more congenial setting for human activity—the convoluted seaboard of southeastern Alaska and British Columbia, where forested islands formed a barrier against the open ocean, creating a protected inland waterway. Several major rivers sliced through the coastal mountains there, draining large areas of the interior, and many smaller streams carried glacial melt to the ocean. Below the largest of the coastal islands—known to posterity as Vancouver—stretched the straight shores of Washington State and Oregon, broken here and there by bays or estuaries. Some of the openings, like that at the mouth of the Columbia River, were quite large; others were mere lagoons, sheltered by reefs. Long, gravelly strands built up along this stretch of the coast, in contrast to the sheer rock that lined the northern sounds.

Once the Ice Age had fully abated, the Northwest Coast was graced with cool summers and mild, wet winters—benefits conferred by the ocean, which moderated temperatures and infused the prevailing westerly winds with moisture. Along most of the coast, the mountains blocked the damp breezes, creating an abundance of misty rain on the western slopes, and leaving the eastern sides relatively dry. Strong storms blew in from the Pacific during the winter, battering the exposed shorelines. Hard freezes were rare in all but the far north, however, and snow seldom covered the ground for long.

Protected from extremes of heat and cold, both sea and shore abounded with life. In the spring and summer months, nearly every river on the Northwest Coast teemed briefly with fish heading upstream to spawn, a recurring miracle that offered a virtually endless supply of food for the inhabitants of the region. Salmon predominated, but there were other species as well—halibut, trout, cod, herring, and smelt. The tidal zone and shallows were abloom with plankton, shellfish, and other marine organisms, which in turn supported an assortment of seagoing mammals, from otters and fur seals to porpoises and whales. The forested mountain slopes rising behind the narrow beaches bristled with fine timber—spruce, hemlock, and cedar—and harbored a profusion of wild animals, including deer, elk, mountain goat, bear, and sleek-coated beaver and marten. In addition to sundry edible roots, the region was home to more than forty varieties of fruits and berries.

The fishermen of the Makah village of Ozette crafted large U-shaped hooks from steam-bent wood and bone barbs to snare the powerful halibut. Smaller straight-shanked hooks with twin barbs caught bass and lingcod.

This inviting realm was not immediately accessible to the nomads who journeyed down from Beringia into the heart of the continent. Ice lingered at the higher elevations of the coastal range and blocked overland access to the Pacific for a time. But by about 8500 BC, Indians had evidently traveled through passes in the mountains to the forests of Oregon and Washington State and were tracking prey there with stone points. Members of these hunting bands also made needles and other instruments out of animal bones, and beads and pendants from various kinds of shells.

Beginning in approximately 8000 BC, other adventurers infiltrated the Northwest Coast by making their way down from Alaska, probably using dugout canoes to navigate the generally peaceful waters separating the offshore islands from the mainland. The pioneers who migrated south along this route brought with them distinctive tools, including so-called microblades that were probably wedged into hafts made of wood or antler to form knives for dressing fish and other delicate tasks. In addition, the coastal Indians fashioned implements from large rounded pebbles, which were coarsely flaked at the bottom to form choppers that fit neatly in the palm of the hand and must have proved useful for woodworking; conceivably, the people who plied the protected waters employed them to carve the hulls of their dug-

Rocky tidal pools have for many centuries supplied the people residing on the Northwest Coast with bountiful year-round provisions, including clams, mussels, sea anemones, limpets, and goose barnacles.

A descendant of the ancient Indians of the Pacific Northwest, a Kwakiutl woman wearing a traditional cedar-bark cloak and broad-brimmed hat gathers abalone along the coast of British Columbia.

outs. From encampments located along the Strait of Georgia and Puget Sound, some Indians who were equipped with such tools ventured upstream to harvest the spawning salmon, leaving the distinctive implements behind at their major fishing sites along the Columbia and Fraser rivers.

All through the Northwest, these early foragers lived in small groups, each of them mobile within its own domain, moving seasonally in pursuit of fish, game, and other sustenance. Gradually, their exploitation of the region's resources became more systematic and effective, and most of the bands looked increasingly to the rivers and the sea for their livelihood. Not only was the tracking of elusive prey in rough, forested terrain more difficult than fishing, but the resources of the shore and ocean were less affected by seasonal changes. Shellfish could be harvested throughout the year, and bottom fish were available to the people between salmon runs. As a result, the majority of the bands elected to settle near the shore, establishing regular coastal bases from which they ventured periodically to forage for food in other locations. The proximity of rich beds of shellfish was a great incentive for settlement. By 3000 BC some beds were being worked by so many Indians from the surrounding area that prominent mounds of discarded shells arose—middens that still mark the landscape today.

When not gathering shellfish or extracting the meat, the coastal Indians cut timber with stone adzes that had been ground and polished to a fine edge, and worked the wood with a variety of tools to create canoes, containers, and other necessities. Plying their canoes, they drew further nourishment from the rivers or bays with hook and line, and harpoon heads crafted of wood, bone, or antler. So prolific were the waters that the Indians in some places derived nearly all the protein they required from fish and sea mammals.

Here, as in the Southwest and the eastern woodlands, the development of techniques for preserving food helped foster larger and more stable communities—although the practice of moving to seasonal camps continued. People who were living along the coast learned to generate reserves for their households by smoking and drying salmon and other fish that swarmed up the inlets periodically. This capability helped promote the growth of substantial villages, whose residents still foraged far from their home base when the occasion arose but whose stores of food were generally sufficient to make it possible for them to devote considerable time and energy to handiwork and other cultural pursuits.

A long, narrow strip of rugged coastline that extends from present-day southeastern Alaska to northern California has been home to communities of native peoples for thousands of years. Collectively called the Northwest Coast Indians, they settled on the shore, or along rivers and creeks that were fed by melting glaciers of the nearby mountain ranges. Theirs was a land of plenty, with a benign climate and a bounty of marine and animal life. Descendants of the original inhabitants make up some of the tribes designated at right.

Few traces of these early villages have survived in the damp environment of the Northwest Coast, where untended wooden structures and implements quickly crumble. Nonetheless, enough evidence has been salvaged in the form of tools, building sites, and the remains of food supplies and the villagers themselves to convey the basic outlines of the maritime culture. By all indications, it was a prosperous existence, so well adapted to the environment that life in towns settled as early as 500 BC was probably not radically different from that in Ozette 2,000 years later.

The smallest settlements might have had no more than 50 inhabitants, but some large villages, spreading across several acres, accommodated as many as 1,000. The heavy-timbered cedar-plank houses were generally large enough to hold several related families. The average dwelling was 30 feet wide and 60 feet long, and many were more than double that size; in some cases, an entire village might live in a row of contiguous houses with separate entrances that extended for up to 1,000 feet. Houses were usually arrayed along a beach suitable for launching heavy canoes, often an estuary or bay, attractive for its relatively quiet waters and varied food resources.

Proximity to a salmon-fishing site was important, but not paramount, since smoked or dried salmon could be transported to a village established in a more sheltered location, or in a place that provided access to other assets, such as trade routes or sea mammal hunting grounds. In the more exposed parts of the coast, Indians might establish their main base well back on an inlet as insurance against winter storms; the residents might then move to another camp close to the sea during the summer. Houses were often built to be disassembled, and some villagers shifted base three or more times a year.

Wherever the community was centered, its most important resources were its fisheries—chiefly the rivers where quantities of salmon appeared every summer to spawn. The salmon gave of their flesh so freely that tribes that later inhabited the region portrayed them in legends as immor-

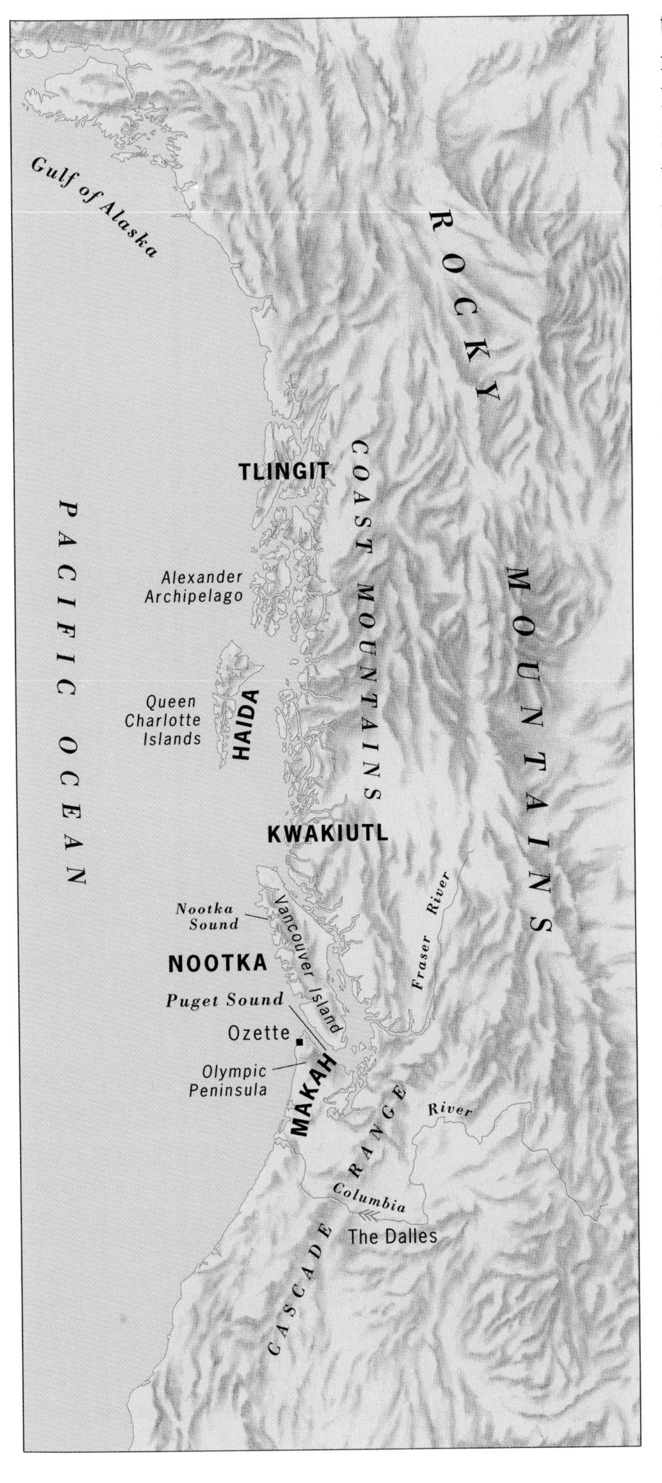

tals who sacrificed their bodies in order to feed humans. At a typical salmon run, fishermen assembled latticelike wooden weirs across the river to divert the fish from their upstream course while allowing the water to flow past. The confined salmon were easy prey for men whose hunting gear had been perfected for millennia. Leisters with barbed prongs ensured that a writhing fish could not free itself. For the heavier quarry such as chinook salmon, which could grow to a weight of forty pounds or more, the Indians resorted to bone-tipped harpoons with long shafts that allowed accurate stabs. Once the point penetrated the target, it separated from its shaft, and the fisherman then tugged on a line of sinew that was attached to the point to retrieve the big catch, whose struggles might otherwise snap or dislodge a rigid shaft. Dip nets made of nettle twine were also used on occasion to scoop smaller fish from the river.

No sooner were the fish tossed ashore than they were cleaned in preparation for drying or smoking. The bones were left in until the fish was consumed. Sometimes after feasting on the catch, people threw salmon bones back into the water to allow the spirit of the fish to return to the sea for reincarnation so that the salmon would come back to their river in abundance the next summer.

In tidal zones, the Indians devised ingenious stone traps—walls that were covered by water at high tide, permitting the fish to swim over them, only to be caught within when the tide fell; extending for more than 100 yards in some instances, the walls were carefully maintained for many generations. Meanwhile, hunters who had ready access to migratory whales and seals developed distinctive techniques of their own. In the spring, whalers in forty-foot canoes carrying several men ranged as far as twenty miles out to sea—well beyond sight of land—to confront whales that were as long as their boats and substantially heavier, up to forty tons. Towed laboriously back to

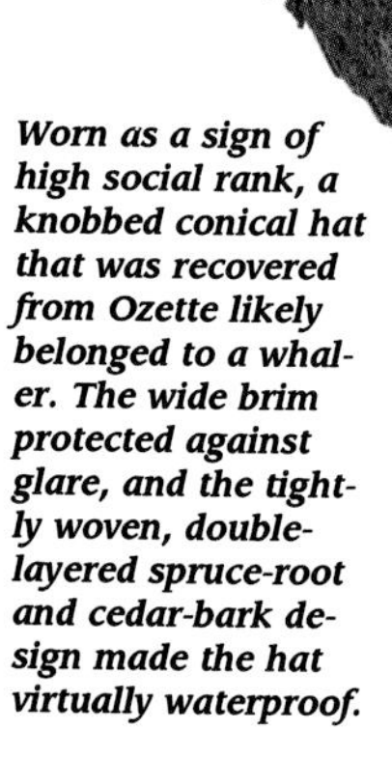

Worn as a sign of high social rank, a knobbed conical hat that was recovered from Ozette likely belonged to a whaler. The wide brim protected against glare, and the tightly woven, double-layered spruce-root and cedar-bark design made the hat virtually waterproof.

the beach, the huge carcasses were then butchered in a process that left little behind. In addition to the whale blubber, which was rendered for its oil, there was meat for the larder. The intestines were turned into containers, the sinews were braided into rope, and the bones became tools.

These maritime cultures relied to a great degree on materials drawn from the nearby forests—huge cedar logs that were hollowed out for canoes; plant fibers that were twined into ropes, lines, and nets; bark and roots that were woven into mats, bags, hats, and storage baskets. The carpenters living on the coast worked wonders with their simple tools, helped along by obliging materials. Red cedar, for example, was so easily cut and split into planks that Northwestern Indian lore celebrated the tree as a generous spirit that, like the salmon, longed to be used. And used it was—felled, split, shaped, and carved with stone adzes, hardwood wedges, bone drills, and other implements.

The craftsmanship that went into making common wooden storage boxes demonstrated the ingenuity of the carpenters. Most of the boxes were made from a single cedar plank, with three deep grooves scored across its surface. The plank was first steamed to make it pliable, then bent at the grooves to form a box with three seamless corners; the fourth corner was sewn shut. The bottom of the container consisted of another plank, which had been rabbeted around its edges for a snug fit. Wooden pegs were driven into carefully drilled holes to secure the bottom, and all the joints were sealed with a clamshell paste. Such watertight coffers, equipped with snug lids, served as receptacles for everything from fish oil to ceremonial garments. These storage boxes, along with various wooden weapons, tools, and ornaments, were often elaborately carved or painted, sometimes with likenesses of humans or animals, sometimes with geometric patterns. The artisan generally used a beaver-tooth knife or chisel for fine carving.

The wealth of the region made it possible for most villages to remain economically independent, with little need for trade in subsistence goods, although some of the tribes exchanged their surplus catch for stone or other items offered to them by traders from the interior. The Columbia River, a hugely productive salmon fishery that supported a population of

THE SPIRIT WITHIN THE KILLER

From age to age, the Northwest Coast Indians have told stories of the killer whale's great physical strength, and of a spirit, called Scana, who lives in such beasts. A tale from the Haida people of the Queen Charlotte Islands depicts Scana's miraculous powers of transformation: It happened that a mischievous band of young men encountered a killer whale while hunting seals and amused themselves by throwing stones at its dorsal fin, injuring the beast. The annoyed whale headed for the beach, where it was mysteriously transformed into a man with a canoe who chided the hunters for breaking his boat. Remorseful, the youths patched the craft, and the man resumed his journey, turning into a whale again as he hit the waves.

As shown below, the story was recorded by a scholar visiting the Haida around 1900; his Haida guide provided the drawing of Scana inside the whale.

Recovered from Ozette, a yew-wood club displays a striking owl's-head carving at either end. Although similar to seal-killing clubs, this finely sculpted weapon shows no sign of wear, suggesting that it may have been used for ceremonial purposes.

about 25,000 people in its lower reaches, also served as an avenue of exchange. Traders carrying goods from as far away as the Great Plains made the journey downriver to meet up with coastal tribes at a thriving marketplace situated near the lowermost rapids on the Columbia—a site known today as The Dalles.

Sometimes, the coastal Indians traded in practical items such as woven broad-brimmed hats, which were coveted as a shield against the frequent rains. But for the most part, they dealt in those alluring raw materials or crafted works that conferred special status upon the owner—treasures fashioned from whalebone, amber, or shiny white dentalium shells collected on the shores of Vancouver Island. These luxury items were usually transported to market in canoes because overland travel was difficult. However, some Indians, particularly those residing to the north, trekked over the mountains to barter with inhabitants of the interior for goods not easily available along the shore, including copper, caribou skins, sinew for thread, and lichen for dye making. The journey across the mountains would have taken them several days in each direction, traversing rocky defiles and icy torrents.

Trade was not the only means of contact between villages in the ancient Northwest; warfare was endemic to at least some parts of the coast. Whether the fights were initiated to gain territory or simply to claim captives who would serve as slaves, they apparently took the form of lightning raids—short, brutal encounters conducted with clubs and daggers. In times of hostility, villagers might move to remote sites, seeking refuge atop rocky knolls or on small, steep-sided islets.

As villages accrued wealth from the immediate environment or from neighboring areas, they evolved prestige systems based on hereditary rank, such as characterized the coastal tribes later encountered by Europeans. Far from passively accepting tribute as their birthright, however, village leaders constantly had to demonstrate their wisdom and generosity. In all likelihood, their duties included managing seasonal activities and setting policy—determining the timing and duration of fishing, hunting, or trading expeditions, for example, or deciding whether to make war or peace with a rival group. And in an economy marked by the sporadic influx of food and other assets, the leaders naturally assumed the role of guarding and redistributing the bounty.

Ancient ceremonies at which leaders doled out surplus resources may have been the origin of the spectacular potlatch ceremonies staged by prominent members of various coastal tribes. The occasion for a potlatch might be the host's claim to a title or some other symbol of rank, which he would assert by presenting gifts to hundreds of invited guests, from his own village and from surrounding communities. That claim would then be validated by the quality and quantity of the gifts he received in return—and the order in which he received them—at a subsequent potlatch given by another leader. Accumulating enough prized goods to stage a proper potlatch encouraged those of high rank to patronize people with special skills, such as carpenters.

By the sixteenth century, when part of Ozette was preserved for posterity by the mud slide, the Makah and other tribes of the Northwest had most likely evolved the sort of hierarchy that was described a few hundred years later by the first visitors from across the seas. The tribal leaders, or titleholders, were the heads of kinship groups. Below them stood the nobility, consisting of their sons, younger brothers, and other close relatives. Nobles might legitimately aspire to a leadership role, provided they inherited the right to a title and could amass sufficient wealth to demonstrate their worth. Commoners, who constituted the largest part of every group, could hold no such hopes, but they were still linked by kinship to their leader and could expect varying amounts of support from him, depending on the services they rendered. Brave warriors or master

Still sleek from the oil that it contained, a man-shaped bowl from Ozette is adorned with a lock of human hair. Vessels carved in human and animal shapes held whale and seal oil for the flavoring of dried and roasted fish.

A replica of a cedar long house (left) copies the windowless plank-and-pole design of original buildings that were excavated at Ozette. Other Northwest Coast communities employed a similar architectural style, as shown in this eighteenth-century watercolor of the interior of a Nootka communal house (below). Under racks of drying salmon, members of the household gather to prepare a meal in a wooden cooking box.

canoe makers were held in higher esteem than simple fishermen, for example.

Slaves occupied the lowest rung on the social ladder. The majority of them were women or children who had been taken in raids against other tribes; captured men were usually killed. Slaves performed menial work for their high-ranking owners, carrying water and firewood and helping with the hunting and fishing. They were no more than property, subject to the whim of their masters; slaves might even be given away or killed to demonstrate the high standing of their master. Occasionally, a slave owner exercised his prerogative more mercifully, granting slaves freedom during a potlatch or some other ceremony.

Such was the profile of village life in the Northwest, garnered from the sites themselves and from the testimony of early witnesses. But not until Ozette divulged its secrets—and those secrets were interpreted in light of enduring Makah traditions—could the culture be appreciated in all its variety.

Ozette, at the time of its catastrophic mud slide, was a thriving example of this rich maritime tradition. Its two rows of houses, the cedar planks of their roofs and sides weathered a soft gray, stretched along a crescent beach that was sheltered from the full force of the Pacific Ocean by a reef as well as by small islands offshore. The houses were sixty to seventy feet long and about thirty-five feet wide. Each dwelling consisted of a heavy, permanent framework made

from hemlock posts, over which the residents laid cedar planks that were secured by flexible cedar withes in such a way that they overlapped like clapboards; when it came time for seasonal moves, the planks could be quickly removed and carried to another framework located elsewhere—in the vicinity of favored salmon fishing grounds, for example. The nearly level roofs of the buildings were painstakingly grooved to channel runoff and were held down either by rocks or by logs. The only openings to be found in the skin of a house were the door and a smoke and ventilation hole in the roof. During wet weather, a sliding wooden panel covered the roof hole, and a woven cedar mat might screen the door.

Jaws agape, a cavorting humpback whale breaks the surface off the Pacific Coast. More docile than the gray whale and yielding nearly twice as much oil, the humpback was a coveted prize for Northwest Indians.

Towering over the houses were twenty-five-foot-high drying racks, which were festooned in the appropriate season with white strips of halibut—the fish that was most plentiful in local waters. The roof of each dwelling might also function as a fish-drying platform during sunny summer weather. Behind the houses stood a variety of specialized structures, including smokehouses for the preservation of fish and sheds for food storage. The shell-littered space between the houses was crisscrossed by an elaborate drainage system that channeled rainwater harmlessly through the village to the shore.

Inside the houses, raised platforms along the walls provided storage and sleeping space for as many as thirty people. These broad benches were made of cedar planks up to thirty inches wide, smoothed with a stone adz. At night, people spread mattresses of cattail reeds for sleeping, and warmed themselves with blankets woven from shredded cedar bark mixed with whatever soft materials were available—downy strips of bird skin, cattail fluff, or dog fur.

The living arrangements were apparently dictated by status. The space directly opposite the door was the place of honor, reserved for the head of the household. The humblest commoners lived next to the entrance. Each family could close off its space with plank walls or woven mats, according to their means. Within these family quarters, wooden chests were used to hold spare clothes, ceremonial regalia, fishing gear, and other personal property.

Cooking took place at family hearths, which were grouped in the center of the house. Fresh fish and meat were roasted on spits of cedar suspended over the fire. Alternatively, a mixture of ingredients—seafood seasoned with berries, for example—might be placed in a wooden box that had been filled with water. Stones hot from the fire were then dropped into the box, bringing the water to a boil. The stew was served in long, trough-shaped wooden dishes.

Partitions between family quarters came down for group activities such as feasting and dancing. On such occasions, hearth fires most likely provided a backdrop for the telling of tales, chanted to the beat of a drum and drawn from a storehouse of legends whose treasures were renewed by each successive generation.

In the winter, when most villagers stayed close to home, the houses became busy workshops. The women crafted baskets for every occasion: small, finely woven bags to hold fishing

A harpoon head created from a mussel shell remains in its cedar-bark sheath some 400 years after it was used by the whalers of Ozette. Imbedded in a whale, the harpoon heads trailed long ropes with attached sealskin floats that tired and slowed the animal so that it could be dispatched with a spear.

A centuries-old mainstay of the Makah diet, filleted halibut are shown drying on towering racks at a summer encampment on Tatoosh Island, off the coast of Washington State near Ozette. On sunny days the fish was air-dried, but in cold or rainy weather it was cured inside a smokehouse.

gear, open-weave pouches for gathering shells and seaweed, or containers so tightly knit they could hold water and be used for cooking or storage. Most of the porous baskets were made from the softened inner bark of the cedar, pulled off in long strips the previous spring when the rising sap made it easy to peel. After they were dried in the sun, the strips were stored in bundles, then thinned and split into ribbons of the desired width, or beaten until they shredded; then they were rolled by the hand against the thigh to yield long, flexible yarns. Watertight baskets and rain hats were usually made from pliable spruce roots, which were washed, partly dried, and split into strips, then woven into a leakproof mesh.

Textiles ranged from heavy, handwoven cedar-bark mats—used as partitions or for wrapping cargo in canoes—to fine, loom-crafted blankets. Loom weaving was a prestigious skill, and some looms were themselves works of art, inlaid with shell and fish teeth. The finest Makah fabric was woven with fur from a special breed of dogs—short, woolly creatures raised expressly for shearing on a small island just offshore. Little time was spent making clothing, for the people were conditioned to the cool moist air and went nearly naked for much of the year. Men wore nothing but ornaments in good weather, while women wore skirts fashioned of animal hides or cedar-bark fabric. There was not even a word for sandals; the Makah went barefoot. When the rains came, they donned their tightly woven hats along with conical capes to shed the water.

The Makah men spent much of the winter making wooden tools and utensils and preparing for the hunting and fishing seasons. Like the weavers, they chose their materials carefully. Mussel shells made strong, sharp harpoon cutting blades, clamped between tough barbs of bone or antler; the composite heads were bound with cherry bark, which shrank when wet. The cedar yarns used in baskets could also be plaited into strong whaling ropes. Bowls for storing and serving food were carved from alder and ash, which had no strong resins that might flavor their contents. Heavy, dense yew was used for clubs, whaling harpoon shafts, and wood-splitting wedges.

Most men in the tribe were able to master the basic carpentry skills required for box making and house construction, but building graceful, seaworthy dugout canoes was a matter for specialists. Ozette obtained some of its canoes in trade from the Indians of Vancouver Island, who were renowned for designs that combined strength, speed, and maneuverability. Most Makah canoes, however, were built in the village—and were held in high enough regard that peoples to the south and east trad-

Following tradition, a Neah Bay carpenter uses an adz to shape the bottom of a cedar-log canoe. After hollowing out the log, the builder softened the wood with boiling water to mold the graceful contours of the hull.

ed for them eagerly. The Makah built canoes in many sizes, ranging from short fishing craft for the use of a single paddler to whaling or war canoes measuring forty feet and longer. A relatively fragile boat was acceptable for travel on rivers or protected waters such as Puget Sound, but venturing into the open sea in search of whales required sturdier vessels that could stand up to a heavy swell.

Whatever its design, the basic construction principles of a canoe were the same. The builder began by felling a large red cedar in the depths of the forest, where the trees grew straight and knot free. He stripped it of branches and split it in half lengthwise with wedges driven by a stone maul. A crew of men then dragged the rough hull to the village beach, where the builder began working first on the round side, using an adz and wedges to shape the exterior of the canoe. Then he turned the log over and used the same tools to hollow out the interior. By the end of this laborious process, the bottom of the shell was about two fingers'

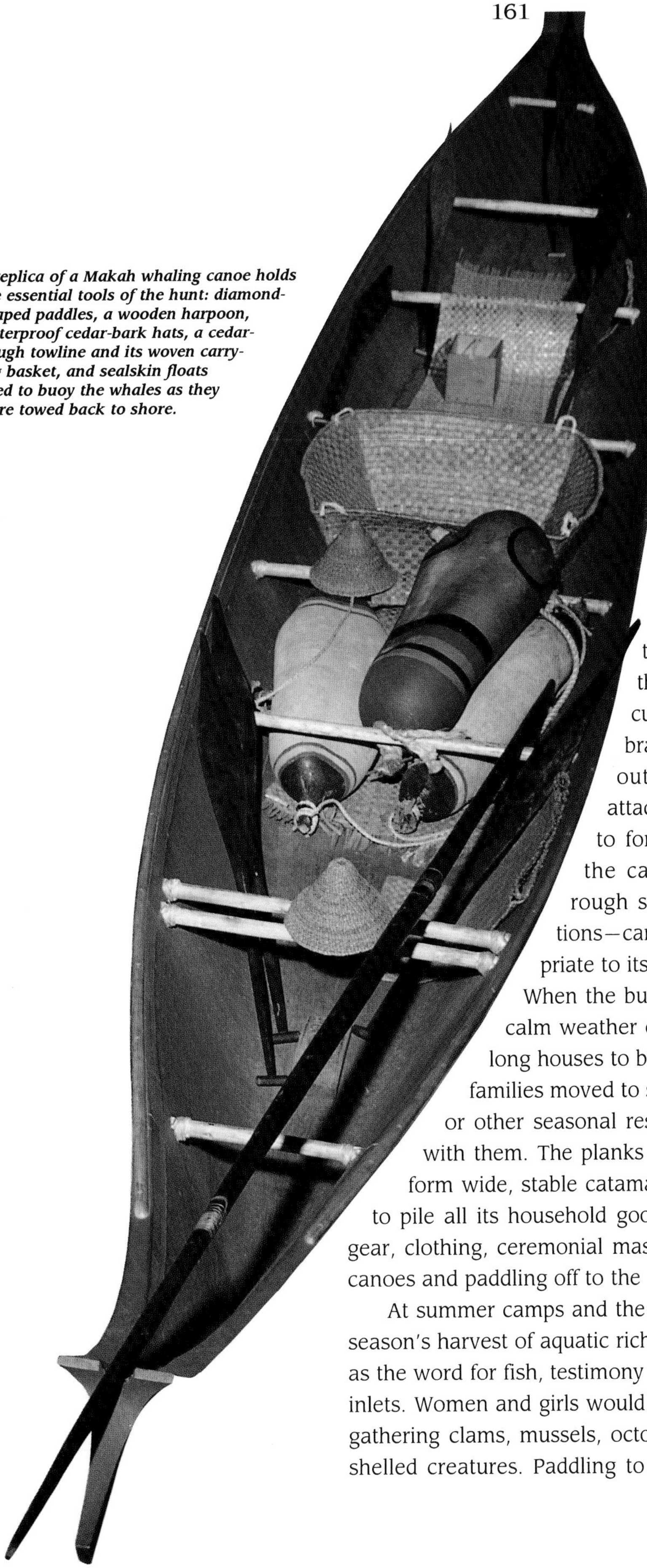

A replica of a Makah whaling canoe holds the essential tools of the hunt: diamond-shaped paddles, a wooden harpoon, waterproof cedar-bark hats, a cedar-bough towline and its woven carrying basket, and sealskin floats used to buoy the whales as they were towed back to shore.

width thick, tapering to a single finger thickness at the top rim. Next, the craftsman filled the canoe with water, which he brought to a boil by adding hot rocks; fires kindled nearby heated the exterior. When the wood had been suitably softened by the wet heat, he widened the canoe by bending the sides outward and installing thwarts across the interior.

Most of the seagoing canoes were fitted with high bow and stern pieces for protection against waves. The builder carved these pieces so precisely that when he secured them with cedar dowels or spruce-branch lashings, the fit was watertight without caulking. Long strips of cedar were attached to the rim of the canoe at either side to form gunwales. The builder then finished the canoe by sanding and polishing it with rough sharkskin and adding whatever decorations—carvings, paintings, or inlays—were appropriate to its purpose and the owner's status.

When the buffeting storms of winter gave way to the calm weather of spring, the Makah emerged from their long houses to begin restocking their larders. Some of the families moved to summer residences closer to salmon runs or other seasonal resources, taking their house planks along with them. The planks were lashed across two large canoes to form wide, stable catamarans, atop which each family proceeded to pile all its household goods—mats and baskets, tools and fishing gear, clothing, ceremonial masks, and food—before squeezing into the canoes and paddling off to the summer base.

At summer camps and the main village, the people inaugurated the season's harvest of aquatic riches. The Makah word for food is the same as the word for fish, testimony to their dependence on the ocean and its inlets. Women and girls would comb the beaches and rocks at low tide, gathering clams, mussels, octopuses, sea urchins, and numerous other shelled creatures. Paddling to offshore banks, the men would haul in large numbers of halibut with U-shaped hooks on kelp lines. Throughout the summer months, it might also be possible for them to catch chinook or coho salmon by trolling in the ocean. On bountiful days, thousands of pounds of fish poured into Ozette and its subsidiary camps. Some of it would be eaten fresh, stewed, or roasted; the rest would be filleted and hung on the tall racks to dry.

The beaches, woods, and bogs located around Ozette also were rich sources of foodstuffs that contributed to the diet of the villagers. Women gathered such delicacies as salmonberries, huckleberries, blueberries, cranberries, and strawberries to sweeten their fish stews. The roots of plants and grasses were either steamed or baked in the community's pit ovens. In addition, the forest supplied the settlers with all of the medicines that they needed: a tonic tea of thimbleberry leaves, a toothache cure from salmonberry bark, a poultice of chewed hemlock used to stanch bleeding.

A fan of spruce tied in his hair, a whaler splashes in a chilly pool to spiritually prepare for the hunt. Part of the cleansing ritual involved rubbing the body with hemlock twigs in order to rid it of human taint.

As important as these items were to the Makah, however, the tribe devoted its greatest effort to the pursuit of migratory sea animals. The favorite food of the Makah was the dark, lean meat taken from the northern fur seals, which made their way past Ozette during the month of April, pausing at a feeding ground located just three miles offshore. Lookouts perched atop the rocky islet off the village beach, watching intently for the appearance of the seals. As soon as the sentinels spotted their quarry, they would signal the hunters, who then embarked in their twenty-five-foot canoes, each of them paddled by three or four men.

Approaching the herd in silence and communicating only by hand signals, they watched for sleeping seals floating on their backs. After identifying the unsuspecting prey, the bowman thrust with his long harpoon, which had a cedar-bark rope attached to its head that was tied to two inflated floats made of sealskins. The floats helped to tire the wounded animals, which the paddlers then drew next to the boat and dispatched with a club. So numerous were the seals that they soon filled the canoes; the hunters frequently had to gut them at sea in order to make room for more without swamping the boats.

When hunters dumped the seal carcasses on the beach before hurrying back out to sea, the women began the laborious job of preserving the catch. With practiced hands, they cut the meat into long strips for smoking, and rendered the blubber by boiling it in water-filled canoes and wooden boxes. As the blubber cooked, it released its oil, which the women skimmed off the surface and poured into storage containers that had been made from the tanned stomachs or bladders of sea lions; the oil thus preserved would be used later as a sauce for various dishes.

Given the abundance of fur seal, the Makah paid less attention to other species. However, hair seals that lived in sea caves near Ozette sometimes made up a part of the villagers' diet. The technique employed for capturing these creatures was altogether different. Since a canoe attempting to enter a cave was liable to be smashed against the rocks by the surf, the hunters swam in. To illuminate the caves, they twisted their long hair into topknots that held spruce sticks that had been saturated with pitch. Once inside, a hunter ignited his headlamp with a glowing coal carried inside a hinged shell. The blinded seals scarcely budged from their perches as the hunters scaled the rocks to club them to death.

Whale migrations also began in early spring, but took place farther out to sea than the passage of the fur seals. Gray whales, sperm whales, humpbacks, and right whales bound for the Arctic all did their part to make Ozette one of the most important whaling villages on the coast. Unlike seal hunting, which was open to any Makah man with the requisite skill and strength, whaling was a restricted activity, bound up in wealth and rank. Only leaders and their sons could harpoon whales, and to ensure the purity of the lineage, their only suitable spouses were the daughters of other whalers.

The hunters entered into a cycle of purification rituals long before the first of their prey appeared off the coast. In order to win the cooperation of the whale spirits, the chief whaler and his wife followed a strict regimen, including icy baths in secret prayer pools under the waxing moon, sexual abstinence, and a diet free of the meat of land animals. The whaler's crew was expected to take up a similar ritual a few days or so before the hunt. A difficult or unsuccessful hunt signified improper conduct in some stage of the preparations.

When the hunters finally set out in pursuit of their quarry, the women still had a role to play. The wife of the chief whaler, in particular, had to act out the bond that was thought to exist between her and the whale. She took to her bed, lying immobile in the manner of a docile whale willing to surrender itself to the hunters. She could get up only when she received word that her husband had struck a whale. That news was conveyed by messengers who followed in a canoe close behind the hunters and picked up the harpoon shaft after it broke free of the spearhead lodged in the quarry. The messengers then paddled back to the village ahead of the others, carrying the shaft to the chief whaler's household, where it would stand in honor over his bed.

When the successful hunters beached their catch back at the village, everyone joined in celebration. Songs and speeches praised the whalers and their chief—now adorned, like his prize, with eagle down. The leader claimed for himself the first special cut from around the dorsal fin. Then he doled out six-foot-long slices of blubber to the rest of the villagers, honoring the nobles before the rest. A successful whale hunt brought the community a wealth of oil, bone, and meat. But more than that, it affirmed that the people and their leaders were pursuing the rewards of nature in the proper spirit, and that their age-old compact with the sea and its creatures remained unbroken.

More than 700 sea otter teeth decorate this cedar replica of a whale dorsal fin excavated at Ozette. Presumably a commemorative whaling trophy, the effigy bears the motif of a thunderbird, a creature reputedly able to carry off a whale in its talons, and the image of the thunderbird's helper, a double-headed serpent that represents lightning.

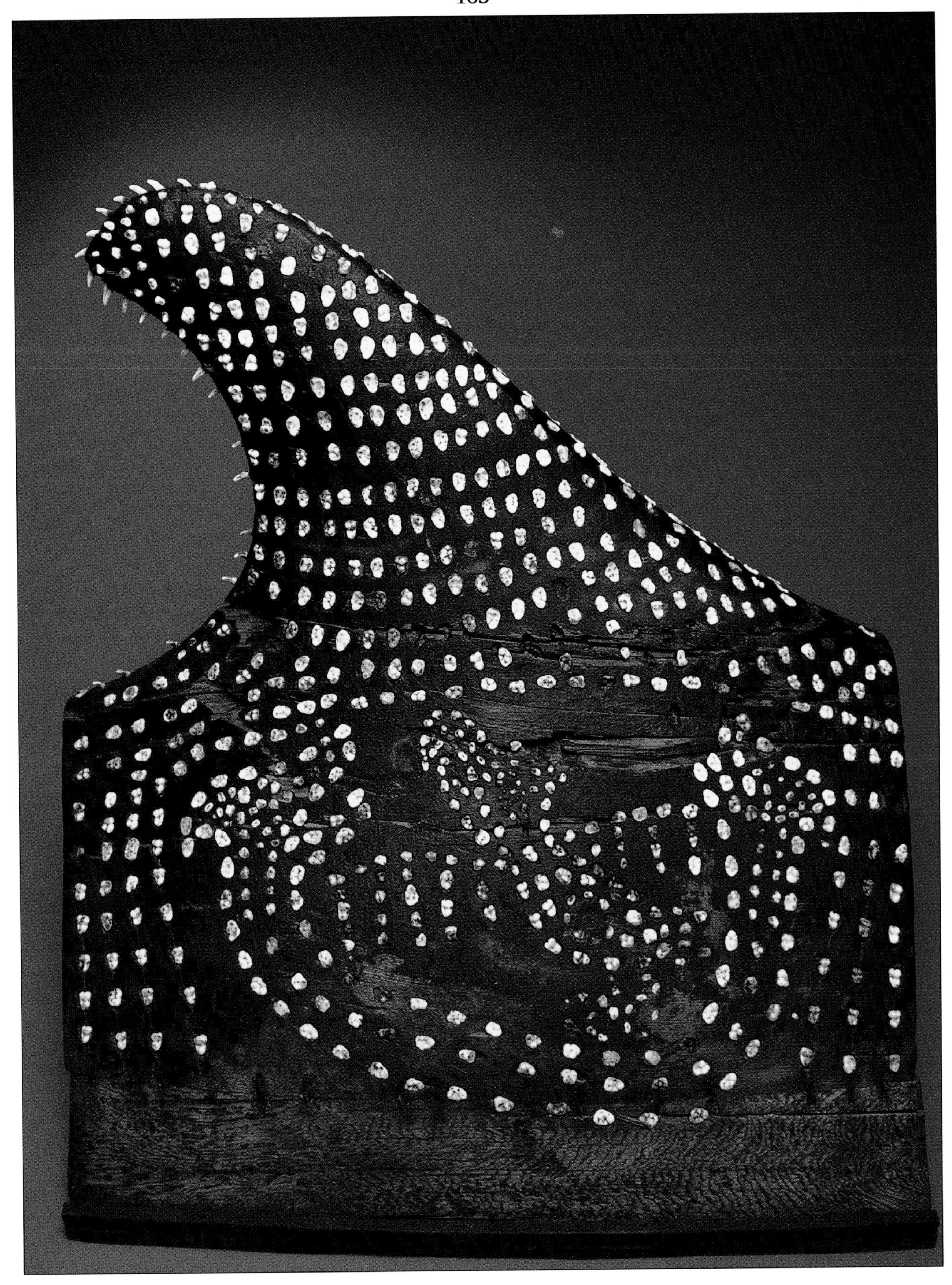

RITUAL AT SEA

Nearly 2,000 years ago, when the arrival of spring calmed and warmed the Pacific Northwest waters, the ancestors of the Makah Indians of Ozette and other villages embarked on a seasonal endeavor, one perilous yet life-sustaining: stalking the great gray whale. These contests between men and the beasts of the sea unfolded in a pattern forged by centuries of repetition and refinement—a ritual that mixed the earthly skills of hunters with evocations of the spirit world.

The time-honored tradition of the whale hunt endured for centuries, until, in the second decade of the twentieth century, the practice dwindled and finally died out. Around 1910, photographers Asahel Curtis and a Makah named Shobid Hunter documented the harpooning, beaching, and butchering of one of the last whales taken at Neah Bay on the Olympic Peninsula. The participants, inheritors of the ancient ways, now wear modern dress and use steel tools instead of bone, but the ritual of the hunt remains unaltered.

Two hunting crews, each with six oarsmen, a helmsman, and a harpooner, set out to find the gray whale. The canoes, made from a single cedar log, were more than thirty feet long and had a high bow and stern as protection against the waves.

A harpooner—by custom a headman or son of a headman—stands in the bow of the boat, poised to thrust the first of several projectiles into the whale. After the spearhead struck home, the hunter retrieved the detachable wooden shaft. Fastened to each spearhead was a 100-foot-long rope made of cedar bark with four sealskin floats that slowed the animal in its flight and sapped its strength.

Victorious hunters float their prize toward the village beach. The leviathans weighed as much as forty tons; towing one from the hunting grounds to shore took every ounce of the paddlers' strength. After numerous harpoon wounds and the drag of the seal-skin floats had exhausted the whale, the hunters immobilized it by slashing the great tendons of the tail. While the creature splashed helplessly in the water, they struck the final blow, driving a bone-tipped (or, in more recent times, a metal-tipped) lance into the heart. A diver then sewed the animal's mouth shut with the cedar-bark towline in order to seal in buoyant gases and prevent water from sinking the carcass as it was brought to shore. The sealskin floats, which were still attached to the harpoon points embedded in the whale, now helped to keep it above water. In the event of an accident, the floats also served as life preservers for the whale hunters.

Makah villagers of all ages help beach the catch. The entire community gathered to welcome both whale and hunters, and to praise the spiritual power that made the hunt successful. Before butchering the carcass, a whaler (inset) peels away skin to remove embedded harpoon points. Each point bore a unique design to ensure that the proper harpooner was credited with the kill.

While the men attend to the body of the whale at water's edge, women sitting on the beach pray for its spirit. The group's spiritual involvement in the hunt was considered as crucial to its success as the strength and skill of the hunters. Tribal members offered various invocations to entice the souls of the animals, such as the following: "Whale, I have given you what you wish to get, my good harpoon. Please hold it with your strong hands. Tow me to the beach of my village, for when you come ashore there, young men will cover your great body with bluebill duck feathers and with the down of the great eagle."

Villagers surround the beached whale, cutting off the blubber in huge slabs with a chisel-like knife called a "būtūk." Workers pulling on lines attached to each section helped strip off the slabs. The whale was measured and distributed according to rigid rules, with the principal harpooner retaining possession of the oil-rich saddle around the dorsal fin. The Makah used virtually every part of the animal; they even ate the skin, which was considered a delicacy.

ACKNOWLEDGMENTS

The editors wish to thank the following individuals and institutions for their valuable assistance in the preparation of this volume:

Alabama: Tuscaloosa—James Knight, University of Alabama.

Arizona: Flagstaff—Carol T. Burke, Linda Eaton, Museum of Northern Arizona.

California: Los Angeles—Richard Buchen, Philip J. Huld, Craig Klyver, Southwest Museum. San Diego—Ken Hedges, Museum of Man.

Illinois: Evanston—James Brown, Northwestern University.

Washington, D.C.: Dennis Stanford, Museum of Natural History, Smithsonian Institution.

Washington State: Neah Bay—Keely M. Parker, Maria Pascua, Makah Cultural and Research Center. Seattle—Richard H. Engeman, Sandra Kroupa, Carla Rickerson, University of Washington Libraries; Stan Shockey, University of Washington. Tacoma—Ruth Kirk; Elaine Miller, Joy Werlink, Washington State Historical Society.

BIBLIOGRAPHY

BOOKS

Adams, E. Charles, *The Origin and Development of the Pueblo Katsina Cult.* Tucson: University of Arizona Press, 1991.

Ambler, J. Richard, *The Anasazi: Prehistoric People of the Four Corners Region.* Flagstaff: Museum of Northern Arizona, 1989.

Amsden, Charles Avery, *Prehistoric Southwesterners from Basketmaker to Pueblo.* Los Angeles: Southwest Museum, 1949.

Andrews, Ralph W., *Indian Primitive.* New York: Bonanza Books, 1960.

Anthropological Society of Washington, *New Interpretations of Aboriginal American Culture History.* New York: Cooper Square Publishers, 1972.

Baity, Elizabeth Chesley, *Americans before Columbus.* New York: Viking Press, 1951.

Barnett, Franklin, *Dictionary of Prehistoric Indian Artifacts of the American Southwest.* Flagstaff, Ariz.: Northland Press, 1973.

Billard, Jules B., ed., *The World of the American Indian.* Washington, D.C.: National Geographic Society, 1979.

Broder, Patricia Janis, *Shadows on Glass: The Indian World of Ben Wittick.* Savage, Md.: Rowman & Littlefield Publishers, 1990.

Brody, J. J.:
The Anasazi: Ancient Indian People of the American Southwest. New York: Rizzoli, 1990.
Mimbres Painted Pottery. Santa Fe, N.Mex.: School of American Research, 1977.

Brody, J. J., Catherine J. Scott, and Steven A. Le Blanc, *Mimbres Pottery: Ancient Art of the American Southwest.* New York: Hudson Hills Press, 1983.

Brown, Virginia Pounds, and Helen Morgan Akens, *Alabama Heritage.* Huntsville, Ala.: Strode Publishers, 1967.

Cameron, Anne, *Daughters of Copper Woman.* Vancouver, B.C., Canada: Press Gang Publishers, 1981.

Ceram, C. W., *The First American: A Story of North American Archaeology.* New York: Harcourt Brace Jovanovich, 1971.

Claiborne, Robert, and the Editors of Time-Life Books, *The First Americans* (The Emergence of Man series). New York: Time-Life Books, 1973.

Coe, Michael, Dean Snow, and Elizabeth Benson, *Atlas of Ancient America.* Oxford, England: Equinox, 1986.

Cordell, Linda S., *Prehistory of the Southwest.* Orlando, Fla.: Academic Press, 1984.

Cushing, Frank Hamilton, *The Mythic World of the Zuni.* Ed. by Barton Wright. Albuquerque: University of New Mexico Press, 1988.

The Editors of American Heritage, *The American Heritage Book of Indians.* New York: American Heritage Publishing Co., 1961.

Fagan, Brian M., *People of the Earth: An Introduction to World Prehistory.* Glenview, Ill.: Scott, Foresman and Co., 1989.

Farb, Peter, *Man's Rise to Civilization as Shown by the Indians of North America from Primeval Times to the Coming of the Industrial State.* New York: E. P. Dutton & Co., 1968.

Fiedel, Stuart J., *Prehistory of the Americas.* Cambridge: Cambridge University Press, 1987.

Folsom, Franklin, and Mary Elting Folsom, *America's Ancient Treasures.* Albuquerque: University of New Mexico Press, 1983.

Frazier, Kendrick, *People of Chaco: A Canyon and Its Culture.* New York: W. W. Norton & Co., 1986.

Frederick, Richard, and Jeanne Engerman, *Asahel Curtis: Photographs of the Great Northwest.* Tacoma: Washington State Historical Society, 1985.

Gerber, Peter R., *Indians of the Northwest Coast.* Transl. by Barbara Fritzemeier. New York: Facts on File Publications, 1989.

Gumerman, George J., ed., *Exploring the Hohokam: Prehistoric Desert Peoples of the American Southwest.* Dragoon, Ariz.: Amerind Foundation, 1991.

Hammack, Nancy S., *Indian Jewelry of the Prehistoric Southwest.* Tucson: University of Arizona Press, 1975.

Holm, Bill, *Spirit and Ancestor: A Century of Northwest Coast Indian Art at the Burke Museum.* Seattle: University of Washington Press, 1987.

Hopkins, David M., John V. Matthews, Jr., Charles E. Schweger, and Steven B. Young, eds., *Paleoecology of Beringia.* New York: Academic Press, 1982.

Hudson, Charles, *The Southeastern Indians.* Knoxville: University of Tennessee Press, 1976.

James, H. L., *Acoma: People of the White Rock.* West Chester, Pa.: Schiffer Publishing, 1988.

Jennings, Jesse D., *Prehistory of North America.* New York: McGraw-Hill Book Co., 1968.

Jochim, Michael A., *Strategies for Survival: Cultural Behavior in an Ecological Context.* New York: Academic Press, 1981.

Jones, Dewitt, and Linda S. Cordell, *Anasazi World.* Portland, Oreg.: Graphic Arts Center Publishing Co., 1985.

Justice, Noel D., *Stone Age Spear and Arrow Points of the Midcontinental and Eastern United States.* Bloomington: Indiana University Press, 1987.

Kirk, Ruth, *Tradition & Change on the Northwest Coast.* Seattle: University of Washington Press, 1986.

Kirk, Ruth, and Richard D. Daugherty:
Exploring Washington Archaeology. Seattle: University of Washington Press, 1978.
Hunters of the Whale: An Adventure in Northwest Coast Archaeology. New York: William Morrow and Co., 1974.

Kopper, Philip, and the Editors of Smithsonian Books, *The Smithsonian Book of North American Indians: Before the Coming of the Europeans.* Washington, D.C.: Smithsonian Books, 1986.

Leach, Maria, and Jerome Fried, eds., *Funk & Wagnalls Standard Dictionary of Folklore, Mythology and Legend.* San Francisco: Harper & Row Publishers, 1984.

LeBlanc, Steven A., *The Mimbres People: Ancient Pueblo Painters of the American Southwest.* London: Thames and Hudson, 1983.

Lister, Robert H., and Florence C. Lister:
Chaco Canyon: Archaeology and Archaeologists. Albuquerque: University of New Mexico Press, 1981.
Those Who Came Before. Globe, Ariz.: Southwest Parks & Monuments Assoc., 1983.

Marr, Carolyn, *Portrait in Time: Photographs of the Makah by Samuel G. Morse, 1896-1903.* Neah Bay, Wash.: Makah Cultural and Research Center, 1987.

Martin, P. S., and H. E. Wright, Jr., eds., *Pleistocene Extinctions: The Search for a Cause.* New Haven, Conn.: Yale University Press, 1967.

Maxwell, James A., ed., *America's Fascinating Indian Heritage.* Pleasantville, N.Y.: Reader's Digest Assoc., 1978.

Moneta, Daniela P., ed., *Chas. F. Lummis: The Centennial Exhibition Commemorating His Tramp across the Continent.* Los Angeles: Southwest Museum, 1985.

Muench, David, *Anasazi: Ancient People of the Rock.* Palo Alto, Calif.: American West Publishing Co., 1974.

Nabokov, Peter, and Robert Easton, *Native American Architecture.* New York: Oxford University Press, 1989.

Noble, David Grant, *Ancient Ruins of the Southwest: An Archaeological Guide.* Flagstaff, Ariz.: Northland Publishing, 1981.

Noble, David Grant, ed., *The Hohokam: Ancient People of the Desert.* Santa Fe, N.Mex.: School of American Research Press, 1991.

Ortiz, Alfonso, *Southwest.* Vol. 9 of *Handbook of North American Indians.* Washington, D.C.: Smithsonian Institution, 1979.

Rohn, Arthur H., *Mug House: Wetherill Mesa Excavations, Mesa Verde National Park - Colorado.* Washington, D.C.: National Park Service, 1971.

Schaafsma, Polly, *Indian Rock Art of the Southwest.* Sante Fe, N.Mex.: School of American Research, 1980.

Silverberg, Robert, *Mound Builders of Ancient America: The Archaeology of a Myth.* Greenwich, Conn.: New York Graphic Society, 1968.

Snow, Dean R., *The Archaeology of New England.* New York: Academic Press, 1980.

Stuart, David E., *The Magic of Bandelier.* Santa Fe, N.Mex.: Ancient City Press, 1989.

Stuart, George E., and Gene S. Stuart, *Discovering Man's Past in the Americas.* Washington, D.C.: National Geographic Society, 1973.

Suttles, Wayne, *Northwest Coast.* Vol. 7 of *Handbook of North American Indians.* Washington, D.C.: Smithsonian Institution, 1990.

Tanner, Clara Lee, *Prehistoric Southwestern Craft Arts.* Tucson: University of Arizona Press, 1976.

Waldman, Carl, *Atlas of the North American Indian.* New York: Facts on File Publications, 1985.

Warner, John Anson, *The Life & Art of the North American Indian.* Secaucus, N.J.: Chartwell Books, 1990.

Waterman, Thomas Talbot, *The Whaling Equipment of the Makah Indians.* Seattle: The University, 1920.

Weatherwax, Paul, *Indian Corn in Old America.* New York, The Macmillan Co., 1954.

Wellmann, Klaus F., *A Survey of North American Indian Rock Art.* Graz, Austria: Akademische Druck-u. Verlagsanstalt, 1979.

Whiteford, Andrew Hunter, et al., *I Am Here: Two Thousand Years of Southwest Indian Arts and Culture.* Santa Fe: Museum of New Mexico Press, 1989.

Wright, Robin K., ed., *A Time of Gathering: Native Heritage in Washington State.* Seattle: University of Washington Press, 1991.

PERIODICALS

Adovasio, J. M., and Ronald C. Carlisle, "Pennsylvania Pioneers." *Natural History,* December 1986.

Bower, B., "Common Origin Cited for American Indians." *Science News,* August 4, 1990.

Bryan, Alan L., "Points of Order." *Natural History,* June 1987.

Claiborne, Robert, "Digging Up Prehistoric America." *Harper's Magazine,* April 1966.

Creamer, Winifred, and Jonathan Haas, "Pueblo: Search for the Ancient Ones." *National Geographic,* October 1991.

Daugherty, Richard D., and Ruth Kirk, "Ancient Indian Village Where Time Stood Still." *Smithsonian,* May 1977.

Fladmark, Knut R., "Getting One's Berings." *Natural History,* November 1986.

"1491, America Before Columbus." *National Geographic,* October 1991.

Frazier, Kendrick, "The Anasazi Sun Dagger." *Science 80,* Premier Issue.

Grayson, Donald K., "Death By Natural Causes." *Natural History,* May 1987.

Guidon, Niède, "Cliff Notes." *Natural History,* August 1987.

Haynes, C. Vance, Jr., "Geofacts and Fancy." *Natural History,* February 1988.

Hillinger, Charles, "Buried Indian Village Called West's Pompeii." *Los Angeles Times,* May 30, 1979.

"Indians Help Excavate Ancestors' 'Pompeii.'" *The Christian Science Monitor,* November 29, 1976.

Irving, William N., "New Dates from Old Bones." *Natural History,* February 1987.

Johnston, David, "Unearthing a Spring Evening Captured Centuries Ago." *Washington Post,* September 4, 1977.

Jonaitis, Aldona, "The Man behind the Indian Masks." *Natural History,* November 1988.

Kirk, Ruth:
"Ozette: The Search Goes On." *Pacific Search,* March 1975.
"Ozette's Indian Legacy." *Westways,* May 1982.

Kirk, Ruth, and Richard D. Daugherty, "Indians and Archaeologists Uncover the Village of Ozette Buried by a Mudslide Centuries Ago." *Historic Preservation,* March/April 1980.

Knebel, Harley J., and Joe S. Creager, "Yukon River: Evidence for Extensive Migration during the Holocene Transgression." *Science,* March 23, 1973.

McCoy, Ronald, "Native America's Legendary Staff of Life." *The World & I,* November 1991.

MacLeish, William H., "From Sea to Shining Sea: 1492." *Smithsonian,* November 1991.

Marshall, Eliot, "Clovis Counterrevolution." *Science,* August 17, 1990.

Martin, Paul S.:
"Clovisia the Beautiful!" *Natural History,* October 1987.
"The Discovery of America." *Science,* March 9, 1973.
"Pleistocene Overkill." *Natural History,* December 1967.

Pascua, Maria Parker, "Ozette: A Makah Village in 1491." *National Geographic,* October 1991.

Pitul'ko, Vladimir, "Ancient Arctic Hunters." *Nature,* January 31, 1991.

Ruhlen, Merritt, "Voices from the Past." *Natural History,* March 1987.

Stanford, Dennis, "The Ginsberg Experiment." *Natural History,* September 1987.

Stuart, George E.:
"Etowah: A Southeast Village in 1491." *National Geographic,* October 1991.
"Mounds: Riddles from the Indian Past." *National Geographic,* December 1972.

Turner, Christy G., II, "Telltale Teeth." *Natural History,* January 1987.

Weaver, Donald E., Jr., "Images on Stone: The Prehistoric Rock Art of the Colorado Plateau." *Plateau* (Flagstaff, Ariz.), 1984.

Wolkomir, Richard, "New Finds Could Rewrite the Start of American History." *Smithsonian,* March 1991.

OTHER SOURCES

Adovasio, J. M., "Pre-Clovis Populations in the New World." (Paper.) Soviet-American Achaeological Field Symposium, U.S.S.R., July 9-23, 1989.

Adovasio, J. M., A. T. Boldurian, and R. C. Carlisle, "Who Are Those Guys?: Some Biased Thoughts on the Initial Peopling of the New World." (Abstract.) Pittsburgh: University of Pittsburgh, 1988.

Amsden, Charles Avery, "Prehistoric Southwesterners from Basketmaker to Pueblo." (Booklet.) Los Angeles: Southwest Museum, 1949.

Bock, Frank G., and Alice J. Bock, "Western Petroglyphs." (Booklet.) El Toro, Calif.: Frank G. Bock, 1974.

Donahue, Jack, and James M. Adovasio, "Evolution of Sandstone Rockshelters in Eastern North America: A Geoarchaeological Perspective." Boulder, Colo.: Geological Society of America, 1990.

Kirk, Ruth, "Makah Cultural and Research Center." (Museum Exhibit Leaflet.) Neah Bay, Wash.: Makah Tribal Council, 1979.

Levenson, Jay A., ed., "Art in the Age of Exploration: Circa 1492." (Catalog.) Washington, D.C.: National Gallery of Art, 1991.

McGregor, John S., "Burial of an Early American Magician." *Proceedings of the American Philosophical Society.* Vol. 86. Philadelphia: American Philosophical Society, 1943.

White, Leslie A., "The Acoma Indians." 47th Annual Report of the Bureau of American Ethnology. Glorieta, N.Mex.: Rio Grande Press, 1973.

PICTURE CREDITS

The sources for the illustrations in this volume are listed below. Credits from left to right are separated by semicolons, from top to bottom by dashes.

Cover: Dirk Bakker photographer, collection of the Saint Louis Science Center. 6, 7: Canadian Museum of Civilization (S75-4047)—Art Wolfe. 8: Library of Congress (Z05198, Z62-52214); Colorado Historical Society. 9-11: Library of Congress (Z05200). 12: Library of Congress (Z05198, Z62-83575). 13: Library of Congress (Z05819); Smithsonian Institution (952A). 14, 15: © Al Grillo/Alaska Stock Images; map by Maryland CartoGraphics, Inc. 16, 17: Art by Greg Harlin of Stansbury, Ronsaville, Wood, Inc. 18: Denver Museum of Natural History. 19: Map by Maryland CartoGraphics, Inc. 20: Southwest Museum, Los Angeles, California (N-22651). 21: Jesse D. Jennings. 22: © Chip Clark, courtesy Smithsonian Institution, Neg. #80-1186. 24, 25: Schenck and Schenck, courtesy Southwest Museum, Los Angeles, California (4)—© Jerry Jacka, courtesy Arizona State Museum, Tucson, Arizona. 26, 27: Jim Brandenburg/Minden Pictures. 28, 29: Art by Greg Harlin of Stansbury, Ronsaville, Wood, Inc. 30, 31: National Museum of the American Indian, Smithsonian Institution (3242). 32, 33: National Museum of Anthropology and History, Mexico City, Mexico; © Walter H. Hodge/Peter Arnold, Inc. 34: Arizona State Museum, Tucson, Arizona—Southwest Museum, Los Angeles, California; Schenck and Schenck, courtesy Southwest Museum, Los Angeles, California. 35: © Jerry Jacka. 36, 37: © Jerry Jacka—Gene Balzer, courtesy Museum of Northern Arizona, Flagstaff, Arizona (E9646); Werner Forman Archive, London/The Schindler Collection, New York. 38, 39: © Richard Alexander Cooke III, inset by Ira Block. 40: © John Running 1989. 42: © Jerry Jacka, courtesy Arizona State Museum, Tucson, Arizona. 44, 45: David Muench. 47: Map by Maryland CartoGraphics, Inc. 48: Museum of New Mexico (27184). 51: Jerry Howard, Pueblo Grande Museum—Schenck and Schenck, courtesy Southwest Museum, Los Angeles, California. 52: Arizona State Museum, Tucson, Arizona (C-1433c). 53: © Jerry Jacka, courtesy Arizona State Museum, Tucson, Arizona. 54, 55: Art by Greg Harlin of Stansbury, Ronsaville, Wood, Inc. 56, 57: Art by Will Williams of Stansbury, Ronsaville, Wood, Inc.—© Jerry Jacka (5). 58: David Muench; Karl Kernberger. 59: Art by Fred Holz. 61: © Richard Alexander Cooke III, courtesy National Museum of the American Indian, Smithsonian Institution. 62: © Tom Till, inset art by Will Williams of Stansbury, Ronsaville, Wood, Inc. 64, 65: Tom Baker—art by Rob Wood of Stansbury, Ronsaville, Wood, Inc. 67: Museum of New Mexico (16039). 68, 69: Library of Congress (Z06453, Z62-46879)—Library of Congress (Z06453, Z62-80165); Southwest Museum, Los Angeles, California. 70: Southwest Museum, Los Angeles, California. 72, 73: Southwest Museum, Los Angeles, California. 74, 75: David Muench. 76: David Muench. 77: Laurence E. Parent—David Muench. 78: David Muench. 79: Ira Block. 80: George H. H. Huey. 81: David Muench. 82, 83: © Tom Till. 84: Willard Clay; Laurence E. Parent. 85: George H. H. Huey. 86: David Muench. 87: © Tom Till. 88, 89: © Jerry Jacka. 90: The Brooklyn Museum 03.325.11655, museum expedition 1903/purchased with funds given by A. Augustus Healy and George F. Peabody, © Justin Kerr—Robin Stancliff, courtesy of Amerind Foundation, Inc.—Trans. #4482, photo by Denis Finnin, courtesy Department of Library Services American Museum of Natural History—Grants Chamber of Commerce Museum. 91: Item #1151, Douglas Kahn, photographer, Museum of Indian Arts and Culture/Laboratory of Anthropology, Santa Fe, New Mexico; © Jerry Jacka, courtesy Arizona State Museum, Tucson, Arizona. 92: © Jerry Jacka—© Richard Alexander Cooke III, courtesy Mesa Verde National Park, National Park Service—© Jerry Jacka (2). 93: Southwest Museum, Los Angeles, California—Arizona State Museum, Tucson, Arizona (2)—© Richard Alexander Cooke III, courtesy Arizona State Museum, Tucson, Arizona; © Richard Alexander Cooke III, courtesy Chaco Cultural National Park. 94, 95: Item #8249, Douglas Kahn, photographer, Museum of Indian Arts and Culture/Laboratory of Anthropology, Santa Fe, New Mexico—© Jerry Jacka, courtesy The Heard Museum, Phoenix, Arizona; Item #43321, Mary Peck, photographer, Museum of Indian Arts and Culture/Laboratory of Anthropology, Santa Fe, New Mexico; © Jerry Jacka (2)—© Richard Alexander Cooke III, courtesy National Park Service. 96: © Richard Alexander Cooke III. 99: Map by Maryland CartoGraphics, Inc. 100, 101: Dirk Bakker, Ohio Historical Society—art by L. K. Townsend, courtesy Cahokia Mounds State Historic Site. 103: Ohio Historical Society. 104, 105: Effigy Mounds National Monument; George Gerster/Comstock. 106: Ohio Historical Society; © Richard Alexander Cooke III, courtesy Ohio Historical Society (2). 107: Peabody Museum, Harvard University, photo by Hillel Burger; Ron Testa/Field Museum of Natural History (A-110015c). 109: Map by Maryland CartoGraphics, Inc., inset photos, Field Museum of Natural History (56784); Ohio Historical Society—Field Museum of Natural History (A110028c)—Field Museum of Natural History (A110017c)—© Richard Alexander Cooke III, courtesy Ohio Historical Society—Field Museum of Natural History (A110017c). 110: Art by Greg Harlin of Stansbury, Ronsaville, Wood, Inc. 111: Art by Rob Wood of Stansbury, Ronsaville, Wood, Inc. 112: Ohio Historical Society—The Thomas Gilcrease Institute of American History and Art, Tulsa, Oklahoma. 113: Ohio Historical Society—National Museum of the American Indian, Smithsonian Institution (1533). 114, 115: Milwaukee Public Museum (70404); The Saint Louis Art Museum (34:1953). 116, 117: National Museum of the American Indian, Smithsonian Institution (2574); National Museum of the American Indian, Smithsonian Institution (2584). 118, 119: © Richard Alexander Cooke III, courtesy National Museum of the American Indian, Smithsonian Institution. 120, 121: Dirk Bakker, Detroit Institute of Arts. 123: © Richard Alexander Cooke III, courtesy National Museum of the American Indian, Smithsonian Institution. 124: Dirk Bakker, Detroit Institute of Arts (712, WL-64); © Richard Alexander Cooke III, courtesy University of Alabama State Museum of Natural History—University of Arkansas (32-74-129). 125: Richard Alexander Cooke III, courtesy University of Alabama State Museum of Natural History—National Museum of the American Indian, Smithsonian Institution (2310); National Museum of the American Indian, Smithsonian Institution (4428). 126: Smithsonian Institution (82-12158). 128: Smithsonian Institution (1168-B-2). 129: National Museum of the American Indian, Smithsonian Institution (2660). 130, 131: David Muench. 132: David Weintraub/Photo Researchers—Wally MacGalliard—Ira Block; David Muench—Jim Zintgraff. 133: Ira Block. 134, 135: David Muench; Frank and A. J. Bock—Ira Block. 136, 137: Richard Parker/Photo Researchers—Wally MacGalliard; Jim Brandenburg/Minden Pictures—Ruth and Louis Kirk; Wally MacGalliard. 138, 139: David Muench. 140: © Richard Alexander Cooke III, courtesy Makah Cultural and Research Center. 142, 143: © Richard Alexander Cooke III; Ruth and Louis Kirk, courtesy Makah Cultural and Research Center. 144: Special Collections Division, University of Washington Libraries, Edward S. Curtis photo (NA 482). 145: © Richard Alexander Cooke III, courtesy Makah Cultural and Research Center. 146, 147: Jim Brandenburg/Minden Pictures; Library of Congress. 149: Map by Maryland CartoGraphics, Inc. 150: Ruth and Louis Kirk, courtesy Makah Cultural and Research Center. 151: James G. Swan Papers, University of Washington Libraries, photo by Stan Schockey. 152: Ruth and Louis Kirk, courtesy Makah Cultural and Research Center. 153: © Richard Alexander Cooke III, courtesy Makah Cultural and Research Center. 154, 155: Ruth and Louis Kirk, courtesy Makah Cultural and Research Center; Peabody Museum, Harvard University, photo by Hillel Burger (T325). 156: Michio Hoshino/Minden Pictures. 157: Ruth and Louis Kirk, courtesy Makah Cultural and Research Center. 158, 159: Special Collections Division, University of Washington Libraries, Samuel G. Morse photo (NA 716). 160: Washington State Historical Society, Tacoma, Washington. 161: © Richard Alexander Cooke III, courtesy Makah Cultural and Research Center. 162: Library of Congress. 165: © Richard Alexander Cooke III, courtesy Makah Cultural and Research Center. 166-175: Washington State Historical Society, Tacoma, Washington.

INDEX

Numerals in italics indicate an illustration of the subject mentioned.

O

P

Q

R

S